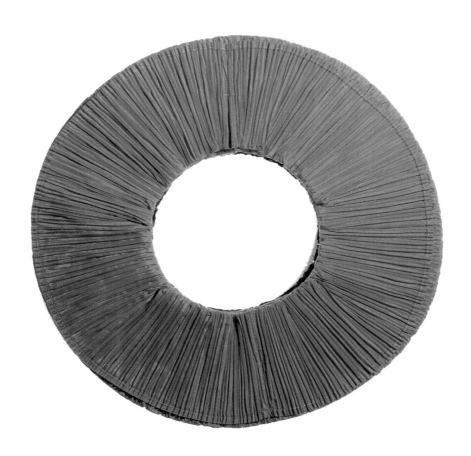

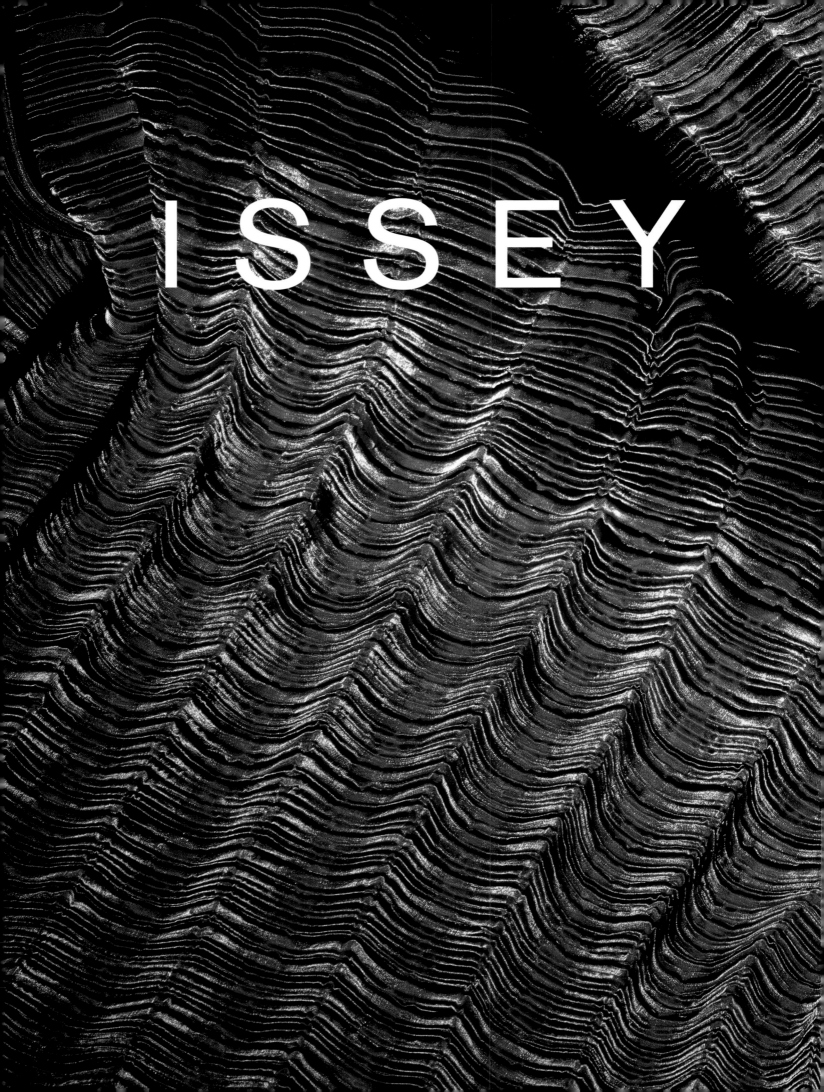

ISSEY

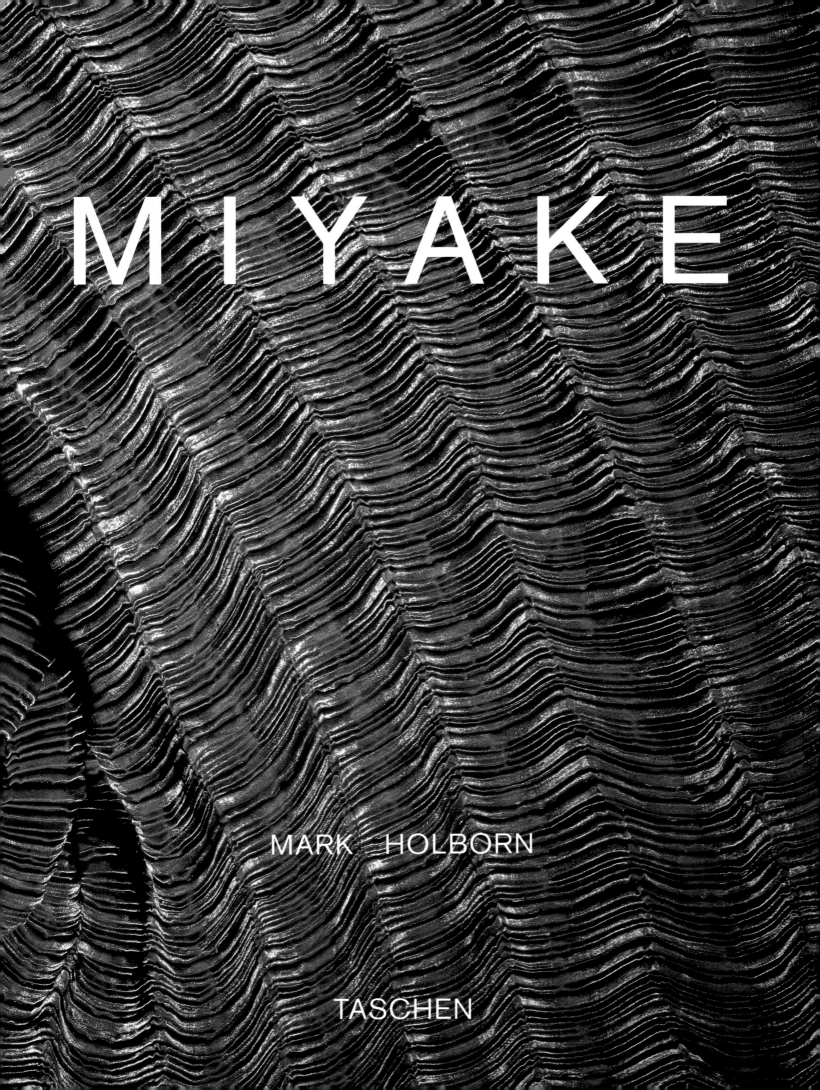

MIYAKE

MARK HOLBORN

TASCHEN

Wave Pleats
Autumn/Winter 1993/94
Photo: Sarah Moon

Issey Miyake, 1993
Photo: Sarah Moon

Page 1 · Seite 1
Flying Saucer
Spring/Summer 1994
Photo: Kazumi Kurigami

Page 2/3 · Seite 2/3
Flying Saucer
Spring/Summer 1994
Photo: Kazumi Kurigami

Page 4/5 · Seite 4/5
Pleats Please
Spring/Summer 1993
Photo: Kazumi Kurigami

Page 6/7 · Seite 6/7
Wave Pleats
Autumn/Winter 1993/94
Photo: Kazumi Kurigami

Page 11 · Seite 11
Flying Saucer
Spring/Summer 1994
Photo: Kazumi Kurigami

© 1995 Benedikt Taschen Verlag GmbH
Hohenzollernring 53, D-50672 Köln
© 1995 Miyake Design Studio, Tokyo
Text © 1995 Mark Holborn, London
Design: Mark Holborn, London; Midori Kitamura, Tokyo
Project Management: Angelika Muthesius, Silvia Krieger, Cologne
German translation: Olga Klenner, Munich
German text edited by Ingrid Loschek, Boxford (MA)
French translation: Joëlle Handley, in association with
First Edition Translations, Cambridge

Printed in Germany
Paperback: ISBN 3-8228-8874-5
Hardback: ISBN 3-8228-8673-4

Paris Collection
Spring/Summer 1994
Photo: Thierry Orban-
Sygma/Imperial Press

Page 12 · Seite 12
Flying Saucer
Spring/Summer 1994
Photo: Kazumi Kurigami

Page 13 · Seite 13
Flying Saucer
Spring/Summer 1994
Photo: Enrique Baduluescu
for *Glamour*

Page 14 · Seite 14
Flying Saucer
Spring/Summer 1994
Photo: Michael Woolley for
Marie Claire bis

Page 15 · Seite 15
Pleats Please
Spring/Summer 1993
Photo: © Miyake Design Studio

Late in 1993 Issey Miyake arrived in London to participate in a series of lectures at a leading art school under the title "Pushing the Boundaries". A week before, he had launched his perfume in America following the showing of his new collection in Paris. A week later, he was to present his collection in Tokyo and travel on to Hiroshima to meet Robert Rauschenberg in connection with the Hiroshima Art Prize, of which he was the first recipient. He is a creative force at the centre of a worldwide commercial enterprise.

"Design is the link between commerce and innovation," Miyake announced at his London lecture. The innovation of his design is conspicuous yet its evolution is entirely consistent. There is a repeated vocabulary to his work, and themes such as pleats develop from year to year as Miyake searches for solutions for practical daily wear. On the one hand, he is highly radical in his invention, following a credo that clothes can be made from anything, and dazzling the fashion viewers with the originality of his design. On the other hand, he is discovering functional, comfortable clothing for the working day. He cites the Walkman and blue jeans as great models of design. His aesthetics are always tempered by function and practicality.

Miyake's influence extends beyond the world of design, attracting comments from architects and even philosophers. He is regarded by many as an artist and his work has been displayed in the controlled setting of the museum installation, yet the work is only completed when his clothes are in motion, vitalized by the human body. He draws inspiration from sculpture, dance, theatre and a view of the human figure. He has absorbed design and colour from the Sudan to Tibet. He emphatically refers to the roots of his craft yet seldom mentions fashion.

"Now in a world where boundaries are being destroyed or re-defined before our eyes, daily, I feel more people are being left without a sense of definition," continued Miyake as he addressed the London students, who were mesmerized by his smile and brilliant red jacket. Apologizing for his lack of linguistic fluency, he proceeded to demonstrate a design revolution as if he was a conjurer pulling tricks from a bag. Dresses appeared out of coiled ropes of brightly coloured cloth or out of crushed balls of fabric. He stretched a flat disc of cloth to form a polychromatic tube – "We call these 'flying saucers'," he quipped. His lecture was a performance as entertaining as it was profound. "I would like to see boundaries remain in the 1990s," he continued, "I think they are even necessary. After all, boundaries are the expression of a culture and history. Instead of the stone walls of the past, I would hope for them to become transparent."[1] His own sense of definition is inescapably rooted in Japan, yet both the inspiration and execution of his work are defiantly international. He is engaged and curious as he criss-

»Grenzen überwinden«: Zu diesem Thema einer Vorlesungsreihe hielt Issey Miyake Ende 1993 einen Vortrag am berühmten Saint Martin's College of Art and Design in London. Eine Woche zuvor hatte er in Amerika sein Parfüm präsentiert, und in Paris war seine neue Kollektion über den Laufsteg gegangen. Eine Woche nach London wird Miyake seine Kollektion in Tokio zeigen und anschließend nach Hiroshima reisen. Dort trifft er anläßlich der Verleihung des Hiroshima Art Prize den amerikanischen Maler Robert Rauschenberg, der diesen Preis als erster erhielt. Issey Miyake ist die kreative Kraft eines weltumspannenden Unternehmens.

»Design ist das Bindeglied zwischen Kommerz und Innovation«, verkündete Miyake in seiner Londoner Vorlesung. Miyakes Innovationen sorgen für Überraschungen, obgleich sie in einer kontinuierlichen Entwicklung stehen. In seinen Kompositionen verwendet Miyake eine eigene Sprache. Strukturen, wie zum Beispiel Falten, entwickelt er, auf der Suche nach tragbarer Alltagskleidung, von Jahr zu Jahr weiter. Einerseits sind seine Entwürfe radikal, wobei er seinem Credo folgt, daß sich Kleidung aus absolut jedem Material machen läßt. Oft verwirrt die Originalität seines Designs die Modewelt. Andererseits entwirft Miyake funktionelle, bequeme Kleidung für den Arbeitsalltag. Als Beispiele für überzeugendes Design nennt er Walkman und Jeans. Seine Ästhetik ist immer mit Funktionalität und Tragbarkeit verbunden.

Miyakes Einfluß erstreckt sich über die Welt des Designs hinaus. Seine Arbeiten erregen die Aufmerksamkeit von Architekten und Philosophen; viele sehen ihn als Künstler. Sein Œuvre wurde in Museen präsentiert und wirkte selbst in der statischen Umgebung einer Ausstellung. Allerdings sind seine Werke erst dann vollendet, wenn sie in Bewegung geraten, zum Leben erweckt werden durch den menschlichen Körper. Die Quellen seiner Inspiration sind Bildhauerei, Tanz, Theater sowie die menschliche Gestalt. Schnitte, Muster und Farben vom Sudan bis nach Tibet fließen in sein Werk ein. Miyake nimmt deutlich Bezug auf die Wurzeln seines Handwerks, selten dagegen gebraucht er den Begriff »Mode«.

»In einer Welt, in der Grenzen gesprengt oder Tag für Tag vor unseren Augen neu gezogen werden, bleiben — meinem Empfinden nach — die Menschen ohne Orientierung, ohne festen Bezugspunkt zurück«, erklärte Miyake den Londoner Kunststudenten, die von seinem Lächeln und seinem leuchtend roten Jackett in Bann gezogen waren. Miyake entschuldigte sich für sein nicht besonders flüssiges Englisch und inszenierte dann eine wahre Revolution im Kleidungsdesign vor den Augen der Studenten, als sei er ein Zauberer, der seine Kunststücke nur so aus dem Ärmel schüttelt. Kleider erschienen aus gedrehten Stoffseilen in leuchtend bunten Farben oder aus zerknitterten Stoffknäu-

A la fin de l'année 1993, dans le cadre d'une série de conférences sur le thème «abolir les démarcations traditionnelles», Issey Miyake s' adresse à des étudiants d'une grande école d'art de Londres. Une semaine auparavant, juste après son défilé parisien, il a lancé son premier parfum aux Etats-Unis. La semaine suivante, il doit présenter sa collection à Tokyo avant de se rendre à Hiroshima pour rencontrer Robert Rauschenberg qui vient de remporter le premier «Hiroshima Art Prize». C'est dire qu'Issey Miyake n'est pas seulement une véritable force créatrice, mais aussi le formidable instigateur d'une opération commerciale de dimension internationale.

«Le dessin de mode, c'est un trait d'union entre le monde des affaires et le monde des arts», déclare-t-il à Londres. S'il est impossible de nier le caractère novateur de ses recherches, son travail progresse toutefois de manière logique et régulière. On retrouve chaque fois la même ligne directrice à travers ses différentes œuvres: ses thèmes favoris (tels les plissés) évoluent d'année en année, à mesure que Miyake adapte ses modèles à la mode de tous les jours. En fait, le créateur nous révèle deux facettes de son caractère: l'inventeur quasiment révolutionnaire qui pense fermement que l'on peut créer un vêtement à partir de n'importe quel matériau de base, et dont les modèles, par leur originalité, éblouissent le public. Mais aussi le Miyake qui découvre le vêtement fonctionnel et confortable, pratique à porter au travail. Pour lui, le Walkman et le jean sont de parfaits exemples de ce que le «design» peut offrir. Sa perception esthétique est toujours tempérée par des accents utilitaires.

L'influence de Miyake transcende les frontières de la mode: avec lui, on peut aussi parler d'architecture et de philosophie. Considéré par beaucoup comme un artiste à part entière, il a vu ses œuvres exposées dans de nombreux musées. Pourtant, ce n'est pas dans ces décors hors de la réalité, souvent rigides, que ses créations prennent tout leur sens, mais bien lorsqu'elles sont portées, vécues par des individus. Miyake puise son inspiration dans la sculpture, la danse, le théâtre, et se laisse guider par une certaine conception de la silhouette humaine. Il s'imprègne des formes et des couleurs qu'il rencontre au hasard de ses voyages à travers le monde, du Soudan au Tibet… Et si on l'entend rarement discourir sur la mode, c'est parce qu'il préfère parler des racines profondes de son art.

«Aujourd'hui, dans un monde où les catégories traditionnelles disparaissent, s'altèrent sous nos yeux, je me rends compte que les gens perdent peu à peu le sens de leur identité» confie, toujours à Londres, Issey Miyake. Les étudiants sont subjugués par son sourire et fascinés par son extraordinaire veston rouge. Après leur avoir demandé de pardonner son «anglais chaotique», il fait planer sur eux ce même souffle révolutionnaire qu'il fait passer sur le monde du design. Tel

crosses the world. His innovation comes not out of a vacuum, but out of the recognition of tradition.

A week after the London lecture, Miyake was in Tokyo graciously greeting friends as they waited for the lights to dim and the new collection to be revealed. The hall was entirely white. Semi-transparent drapes hung from the ceiling in diagonals across a square space. The audience sat to the sides. Cameras were ranged facing the models' entrance. The hall darkened and dancers in white "ethereal" chiffon and taffeta entered to the sound of Mozart.

Miyake, a pioneer of new technology and fabrics, had created a show suggesting primary, elemental qualities. Light, air and breeze were the opening associations in the swirl of transluscent cloth across the white space. Then, from dabs of black on white cloth to slashes of red, colours began to fill the space. After ballooning paper hats came kite-like hats of paper and bamboo and hats in traditional *washi* and oiled papers. There followed a procession of hats of jungle leaves, hats floating on strings, hats like *chochin* lanterns and hats from *Alice in Wonderland*. Designs in chiffon, cotton, mesh-jersey, jute and shrunken *kibira*-linen led to raffia leaves worn as if in some shamanistic rite. The colours of the "flying saucer" dresses formed the climax to the show as the exuberant modernity of the space age followed echoes of ancient culture. In an accompanying programme Miyake referred poetically to make-up inspired by the morning dew, and to hair arrangements like raffia palms in the wind. This deceptive simplicity might suggest that the world of Issey Miyake is a shadowless domain. The models began to dance to James Brown singing "I feel good" and the audience did. Part of Miyake's success is that his work evokes well-being in wearer and viewer alike.

The benign breeze from the Miyake Design Studio in fact originates in the dark ages of modern Japan. Miyake was a seven year-old in Hiroshima, his native city, in August 1945. He is reticent about the details of what he saw in the city and of the subsequent death of his mother. She survived with burns for a further four years from that August, displaying inspirational strength. Miyake's creativity exists not in detachment from the shadows of Japanese history, but in an inescapable response to such experience. His career corresponds exactly to the recovery of the nation, and it is there in Japan, after both Paris and America, that his own sense of definition was established.

Those who spent their childhood during the war years or the bleak, early days of the Occupation are conspicuous as a generation. It is as if the deprivations of the time had spurred some expansive creativity or as if intimacy with ruins had encouraged optimism and engagement with the world. Amongst Miyake's collaborators are the designer, Shiro Kuramata, the art director and designer, Eiko Ishioka, the painter and

eln. Eine flache Stoffscheibe zog er zu einer vielfarbigen Textilröhre auseinander. »So etwas nennen wir ›Fliegende Untertasse‹«, scherzte er. Seine Vorlesung war so unterhaltsam wie sachkundig. »Ich möchte, daß Grenzen auch in den Neunzigern bestehen bleiben«, fuhr er fort, »ich halte sie sogar für notwendig. Immerhin sind Grenzen das Ergebnis von Kultur und Geschichte. Aber statt der Steinmauern der Vergangenheit erhoffe ich mir transparente Grenzen.«[1] Miyakes eigener Bezugspunkt liegt unweigerlich in Japan, aber sowohl seine Inspirationen als auch seine Arbeiten sind eindeutig international geprägt. Engagiert und neugierig reist Miyake durch die ganze Welt. Seine Innovationen entstehen nicht im luftleeren Raum, sondern entspringen der Anerkennung von Tradition.

Eine Woche nach London begrüßte Miyake seine Freunde, die auf den Moment warteten, in dem sich die Lichter verdunkeln und seine neue Kollektion präsentiert wird. Der Saal war vollkommen weiß. Halbtransparente Tücher hingen diagonal über einem rechteckigen Raum. Das Publikum saß an den Seiten. Die Kameras waren auf den Auftritt der Mannequins gerichtet. Der Saal verdunkelte sich, und zu den Klängen von Mozart betraten Tänzer in »ätherisch« weißem Chiffon und Taft den Laufsteg.

Miyake, Pionier neuer Technologien und Materialien, schuf eine Schau, die ursprüngliche, elementare Qualitäten zum Ausdruck brachte. Assoziationen von Licht, Luft und Wind stellten sich ein, als zu Beginn transparente Tücher durch den weißen Raum wirbelten. Schwarze Blitze auf weißem Stoff, gefolgt von Streifen aus leuchtendem Rot begannen, den Raum mit Farbe zu füllen. Das Augenmerk auf die Hüte gerichtet, sah man ballonartige Papierhüte, danach Hüte in Drachenform aus Papier und Bambus, Hüte aus *Washi,* einem traditionellen Reispapier, und aus Ölpapieren. Es folgte eine Prozession von Hüten aus Dschungelblättern, Hüte, die an Fäden schwebten, Hüte, die wie *Chochin*-Laternen (zylinderartige Klapplaternen) aussahen, und Hüte, die an *Alice im Wunderland* erinnerten. Die Kreationen waren aus Chiffon, Baumwolle, netzartigem Jersey, Jute und vorgewaschenem *Kibira*-Leinen, einem ungebleichten, einfach gewebten Hanfstoff, gefolgt von fransenbesetzten Raffiapalmblättern, die an Schamanenrituale erinnerten. Die Farben der »flying saucer«-Kleider bildeten den Höhepunkt der Schau: Die überschäumende Modernität des Weltraum-Zeitalters folgte auf den Widerklang einer frühen Kultur. Im begleitenden Programmheft benannte Miyake poetisch die Quellen seiner Inspiration: der Morgentau für das Make-up, die vom Wind bewegten Raffiapalmen für die Frisuren.

Diese trügerische Schlichtheit könnte den Eindruck erwecken, die Welt von Issey Miyake sei ein Reich ohne Schatten. Die Mannequins tanzten zu James

un magicien sortant des colombes de son chapeau, il exhibe des torsades de tissus aux couleurs éclatantes, des boules de chiffon froissé qui soudain se transforment en robes. Un disque d'étoffe aplati devient subitement un tube polychrome — «l'une de nos soucoupes volantes», plaisante-t-il. Sa conférence se transforme en véritable spectacle, divertissant, certes, mais sans frivolité aucune. «Je ne souhaite pas voir disparaître demain toutes les particularités qui existent aujourd'hui car je crois qu'elles sont nécessaires, l'expression d'une culture et d'une histoire qu'on ne peut renier. Mais je voudrais que les lourdes murailles de pierres d'antan se transforment en cloisons transparentes.»[1] Sa propre identité est incontestablement et profondément issue de la culture japonaise; pourtant, d'inspiration et d'exécution, ses œuvres sont audacieusement internationales. Il parcourt le monde, fidèle à ses engagements et ouvert à toutes les influences. Son talent novateur n'est pas né du néant mais repose bien sur son respect et sa reconnaissance de la tradition.

Une semaine après la conférence de Londres, Miyake accueille ses amis à Tokyo pour leur présenter ses derniers modèles. Dans une salle entièrement blanche, des voilages semi-transparents bruissent au plafond, traversant en diagonale l'espace parfaitement carré. Les spectateurs sont assis sur les côtés et toutes les caméras, disposées à une même extrémité, sont braquées vers l'entrée du podium. Enfin, l'obscurité se fait et des danseurs vêtus de mousseline et de taffetas d'une blancheur onirique font leur apparition. Mozart, aussi, est au rendez-vous.

Miyake, véritable pionnier des nouvelles technologies et des nouveaux tissus, a créé un spectacle qui présente pourtant toutes les qualités élémentaires fondamentales, un univers où des voiles diaphanes ondoyant à travers un espace éthéré symbolisent la lumière, l'air et le vent. Soudain, parmi tout ce blanc apparaissent peu à peu des taches noires, puis des balafres rouges et bientôt les couleurs commencent à envahir l'espace. Les chapeaux eux aussi entrent en scène: chapeaux ballonnés en papier, chapeaux cerfs-volants faits de papier et de bambou, chapeaux traditionnels en papier *washi* et papier huilé, annonçant une procession de couvre-chefs faits de feuilles exotiques, de chapeaux «flottant» au bout de ficelles, de chapeaux aux allures de lanternes *chochin* (lampions pliants cylindriques) ou empruntés à *Alice au Pays des Merveilles*. Les modèles en mousseline, coton, maille, jersey, jute et lin rentré *Kibira* (tissu de chanvre non traité) laissent ensuite la place aux feuilles de raphia frangées, portées à la manière d'un rituel prophétique. Les robes «soucoupes volantes», de par leurs couleurs, forment le «clou» du défilé tandis que l'ère spatiale, exubérante de modernité, résonne encore des échos des siècles passés. Pour compléter le spectacle, Miyake invente des accents poétiques

Spring/Summer 1994
Tokyo Collection
Photo: Fujitsuka Mitsumasa

Page 18/19 · Seite 18/19
Pleats Please
Spring/Summer 1994
Paris Collection
Photo: Philippe Brazil

A Poem of Cloth and Stone
1963, Tokyo
Photo: Kishin Shinoyama

graphic designer, Tadanori Yokoo, and the architect, Tadao Ando. They share a common sense of exploration derived from travel far beyond Japan. Miyake and his colleagues were the first generation of the new Japan, freed from the dogma of pre-war education. Their expansiveness has become part of their identity, overturning critical clichés of Japanese cultural insularity.

The years of Occupation brought not the demonic intruder, as Japanese wartime propaganda had led people to fear, but Mickey Mouse instead. The door was opened on American culture of the Fifties. To Miyake it presented the imagery of America, glorious and confident in its prosperity before the conflicts of the Sixties had surfaced. American cinema and magazine culture, at its grandest and most audacious, invaded Japan. It was the era of the New York art director, Alexey Brodovitch, and of two photographic pioneers, Irving Penn and Richard Avedon, in *Vogue* and *Harper's Bazaar* respectively. Clothes and models were their subjects. Fashion was the language of that culture.

Fashion was not a suitable design study for men in Japan in the Fifties. As a teenager, Miyake had been fascinated by fashion magazines. In 1959 he enrolled as a graphic design student at the prestigious Tama Art University in Tokyo. No independent fashion design course existed. "There was a psychological struggle for me," he recalls, "because fashion had been an area strictly for women. It was a critical question if it would be possible for me. Fashion still meant Paris; Paris of couture collections. I wanted to get past this definition."

Miyake's career as a radical within the design world began the following year, in 1960, when an international design conference was held in Kyoto. Fashion was not on the agenda and Miyake publicly challenged the organizers over the omission. He was determined to establish fashion as a legitimate design study. He received his first fashion commissions from the Toray and Shiseido corporations while still a student. Before his graduation in 1964 he produced a show titled *A Poem of Cloth and Stone* in 1963. "The show is aimed at suggesting clothing as visual creation rather than being utilitarian," he claimed. "We want to stimulate the imagination through clothing. It is not a fashion show, though the works do breathe in contemporary style. Accordingly, I think the next step will be clothing that looks to the future. There are many long dresses in the show, not intended as evening wear but simply for their form. I will be happy if this show becomes the starting point of visual clothing in Japan."[2] Beside his plea for a futurist "visual clothing", his denial of couture was explicit, but before the innovations could begin, he had to establish his foundations.

He arrived in Paris in 1965 to become a student at the Ecole de la Chambre Syndicale de la Couture Parisienne,

Browns Song »I feel good« und genauso fühlte sich das Publikum. Ein Teil von Miyakes Erfolg liegt darin, daß seine Kreationen beim Träger ebenso wie beim Betrachter ein Gefühl des Wohlbefindens auslösen.

Tatsache ist, daß die erfrischende Quelle des Miyake Design Studios den dunkleren Zeiten des modernen Japans entspringt. Im August 1945 war Miyake ein siebenjähriges Kind in Hiroshima, seinem Geburtsort. Er spricht kaum über das, was er damals zu sehen bekam und über den späteren Tod seiner Mutter. Mit schweren Verbrennungen überlebte sie jenen August um weitere vier Jahre, lebte mit einer bewundernswerten Kraft. Miyakes Kreativität existiert nicht losgelöst von den Schattenseiten japanischer Geschichte, sondern als eine unausweichliche Antwort auf jene Erfahrung. Und es ist Japan, nach Paris und nach Amerika, wo sich sein eigener fester Bezugspunkt bildete. In den Kriegsjahren und den trostlosen frühen Jahren der Okkupation wuchs eine bemerkenswerte Generation heran. Es scheint, als hätten die Entbehrungen jener Zeit eine Welle überströmender Kreativität ins Rollen gebracht und die Vertrautheit mit Trümmern einen weltzugewandten Optimismus gefördert. Zu Miyakes Mitstreitern zählen Shiro Kuramata (Designer), Eiko Ishioka (Designerin und Art Director), der Maler und Graphikdesigner Tadanori Yokoo sowie der Architekt Tadao Ando. Sie teilen die Lust am Entdecken und Erforschen, die durch zahlreiche Reisen nach Übersee geweckt wurde. Miyake und seine Kollegen entstammen der ersten Generation des neuen Japans, die nicht mehr durch die dogmatische Erziehung der Vorkriegszeit geprägt war. Ihre Weltoffenheit ist ein fester Bestandteil ihrer Persönlichkeit geworden und widerlegt das Vorurteil, Japan sei gegen alles Fremde abgeschottet. Mit der Okkupation kam kein dämonischer Eindringling, wie die japanische Kriegspropaganda der Bevölkerung glauben machen wollte, — sondern Mickey Mouse. Die Tür zur amerikanischen Kultur der fünfziger Jahre öffnete sich und gab den Blick frei auf ein glorreiches, selbstbewußtes Amerika in voller Blüte. Die Desillusionierung der sechziger Jahre hatte sich noch nicht bemerkbar gemacht. In Filmen und Zeitschriften präsentierte sich die amerikanische Kultur von ihrer großartigsten und kühnsten Seite. Es war die Glanzzeit von *Vogue* und *Harper's Bazaar*, die Ära des New Yorker Art Directors Alexey Brodovitch und der beiden führenden Fotografen Irving Penn und Richard Avedon. Kleider und Mannequins waren ihre Themen, und Mode die Sprache einer Kultur.

Im Japan der fünfziger Jahre war Modedesign als Studienfach für junge Männer tabu. Doch bereits als Teenager faszinierten Miyake die französischen Modezeichnungen. 1959 begann er ein Studium für Graphikdesign an der prestigeträchtigen Tama Art University in Tokio. Ein eigener Studiengang für Modedesign existierte damals nicht. »Für mich war das ein seeli-

grâce à des maquillages «inspirés par la rosée du matin» et des coiffures «semblables à des palmes de raphia doucement balancées par la brise». Cette simplicité est trompeuse et pourrait laisser penser que l'univers d'Issey Miyake est un domaine sans ombre. Lorsque les mannequins se mettent à danser au rythme de «I feel good» de James Brown, tous, acteurs et spectateurs, s'enthousiasment: le couturier sait, par ses créations, procurer une sensation de bien-être à ceux qui les portent, tout autant qu'à ceux qui les admirent.

Ce rayonnement du Miyake Design Studio est pourtant issu de l'une des périodes les plus sombres de l'histoire contemporaine du Japon: Issey Miyake est né à Hiroshima. Au mois d'août 1945, il a sept ans. Il n'aime pas parler de ce qu'il a vu, ni de sa mère, exemplaire de force et de courage, décédée après quatre ans de souffrance à la suite de brûlures de guerre.

L'esprit créateur de Miyake n'est pas le résultat d'une prise de distance par rapport à cette époque ténébreuse, mais le fruit d'une nécessaire réaction à ce type d'expérience. Sa carrière suit très exactement le redressement économique de son pays et c'est au Japon, après Paris et les Etats-Unis, que sa propre identité s'affirme.

Ceux qui ont grandi durant la guerre, ceux qui ont connu la désespérance des premières années d'occupation appartiennent à une génération qui ne ressemble à aucune autre. Il semble que toutes les privations qu'ils ont subies fassent jaillir en eux une créativité débordante, comme si les années passées parmi les ruines et les dévastations aidaient, ensuite, à développer l'optimisme et la foi en un monde nouveau. Les collaborateurs de Miyake (le designer Shiro Kuramata, la directrice artistique et styliste Eiko Ishioka, le peintre et artiste Tadanori Yokoo et l'architecte Tadao Ando) partagent tous une même ardente curiosité, stimulée par leurs voyages bien au-delà des frontières nippones. Miyake et ses collègues font partie de la première génération à découvrir un Japon libéré de ses dogmes isolationnistes. Leur chaleur, leur générosité renversent tous les clichés désobligeants sur l'insularité culturelle du Japon.

Pendant l'occupation, les Japonais ont craint de voir débarquer les démons étrangers que la propagande de guerre leur avait dépeints: mais c'est Mickey Mouse et la culture américaine des années 50 qui arrivent. Miyake aime cette imagerie de l'Amérique d'alors, glorieuse, confiante en l'avenir et sûre de sa prospérité, encore bien loin des drames des années 60. C'est l'âge d'or du cinéma et du magazine, alors à leur apogée. Cette époque consacre également le règne du directeur artistique new-yorkais Alexey Brodovitch et de deux pionniers de la photographie de mode, Irving Penn et Richard Avedon, qui collaborent respectivement à *Vogue* et *Harper's Bazaar*. Ils se penchent sur

*A Tattoo dedicated to the memory
of Jimi Hendrix and Janis Joplin*
Spring/Summer 1970
Photo: Kishin Shinoyama

Page 26 · Seite 26
Tattoo Body
Spring/Summer 1992
Photo: Tyen

Page 27 · Seite 27
Tattoo Body
Autumn/Winter 1989/90
Photo: Tyen

Page 28/29 · Seite 28/29
Textile by Makiko Minagawa
1984
Photo: Tahara Keiichi

he worked first with Guy Laroche and then in 1968 with Givenchy, to whom he is indebted. His entrance into this elegant design world coincided with disturbances leading to the Paris riots of 1968. "My years in Paris were very important as a basis for my career, but the ideas of 'beauty' and the body were too rigid for me," he said. "The ideas were displaced by the freedom of 1968. I couldn't continue with the formality of 'Madame, please'. People were out demonstrating on the streets and I wanted to be party to their struggle. I quit work and hung around for a few months, but I still needed basic training and I joined Givenchy, whom I liked very much. This was my foundation."

At the same time as the disturbances in Paris were occuring, London was thriving in a flamboyant pop culture. On weekends off from Paris, Miyake headed for the King's Road. "The revolution of 1968 made me aware of what I believed in and the validity of those beliefs. Before, passion had existed for special people and special things. I questioned this exclusivity. To me, French culture seemed heavy and cerebral. In contrast I loved the excitement of London and I identified with the spirit of the place. I then gained the self-confidence to continue along the line in which I had always believed. I gained the power to realize a dream for the future."

Miyake's fantasy of America continued in Paris. The New World was the seat of a great popular culture which he viewed from a French perspective. In Paris he learned about the work of Robert Rauschenberg, Claes Oldenburg and Jasper Johns. He left for New York in 1969 with the intention of settling permanently in America. After the sound of the Beatles, he claimed he wanted the intensity of Jimi Hendrix and Janis Joplin – the raw-throated passion of America.

Following six months in the New York studio of Geoffrey Beene, Miyake returned for a short stay in Japan in the winter of 1969 and 1970. He found the country in the throes of enormous transition. 1970 was the year of the Osaka Expo. The global economic axis had shifted. Despite its lack of natural resources, Japan had become a major manufacturing force. Beside the economic recovery came a new sense of cultural confidence. Enormous social sacrifices had been made and there were deep-rooted questions about the nature of Japanese identity. The prevalent Americanization of the Occupation was replaced by the possibility of an independent Japanese culture which accommodated both native and Western traditions with a new modernity. At the Osaka Expo, Tadanori Yokoo designed the Japanese textile pavilion as a building wrapped in scarlet scaffolding on which dummy construction workers were perched beside black crows. The design was a model of the nation at the height of its reconstruction under the gaze of symbols of its past.

scher Konflikt«, erinnert er sich, »denn der Bereich der Mode war ausschließlich Frauen vorbehalten. Es war eine heikle Frage, ob er mir auch zugänglich sein würde. Mode, das hieß immer noch Paris und die Pariser Kollektionen. Ich hatte etwas gegen diese ausgrenzende, überfeinerte Welt und wollte die festgefügten Begriffe aufbrechen.«

Miyakes radikale Erneuerung des Designs begann im darauffolgenden Jahr, 1960, auf einem internationalen Designkongress in Kioto. Modedesign war im Programm nicht vorgesehen, und Miyake kritisierte die Organisatoren öffentlich für dieses Defizit. Er war entschlossen, Modedesign als ein eigenständiges Studium zu etablieren. Schon als Student erhielt er seine ersten Aufträge von Toray und Shiseido. Noch bevor er sein Studium 1964 abschloß, produzierte er 1963 eine Schau mit dem Titel *A Poem of Cloth and Stone*. »Im Vordergrund der Schau steht Kleidung als visuelle Erscheinung; die Nützlichkeit ist in den Hintergrund getreten«, erklärte Miyake. »Kleidung soll die Phantasie anregen. Dies ist keine eigentliche Modenschau, obwohl die Kleider den gegenwärtigen Stil erkennen lassen. Demnach, denke ich, wird der nächste Schritt sein, Kleidung im Stil der Zukunft zu entwerfen. Die vielen langen Kleider in der Schau sind nicht als Abendkleider gedacht, sondern einfach ihrer Form wegen aufgenommen. Ich wünsche mir, daß diese Schau dem visuellen Design von Kleidung den Weg bereitet.«[2] Ebenso deutlich wie sein Plädoyer für »visuelle Kleidung« formulierte er seine Absage an die Haute Couture. Doch bevor er mit seinen Innovationen beginnen konnte, mußte er erst ein Fundament schaffen.

Miyake kam 1965 nach Paris um an der Ecole de la Chambre Syndicale de la Couture Parisienne zu studieren. Von 1965 an arbeitete er bei Guy Laroche, ab 1968 bei Givenchy, dem er sich sehr verbunden fühlt. Sein Eintritt in die elegante Welt der Mode fiel zeitlich mit den Unruhen zusammen, die zu den Pariser Krawallen von 1968 führten. »Die Jahre in Paris waren als Grundlage für meine Karriere sehr wichtig, aber die Ideen von ›Schönheit‹ und Körper erschienen mir zu rigide«, erklärte er. »Diese Ideen wurden durch die Freiheiten der 68er abgelöst. Mit der Förmlichkeit eines ›Bitte, Madame‹ konnte ich nichts mehr anfangen. Die Menschen demonstrierten draußen auf den Straßen, und ich spürte das Bedürfnis, mich an ihrem Kampf zu beteiligen. Ich hörte bei Laroche auf und trieb mich ein paar Monate herum. Mir fehlte es jedoch noch an solider Ausbildung, und deshalb fing ich bei Givenchy an, den ich sehr schätzte. Das war das Fundament meiner Arbeit.«

Während Paris von Unruhen heimgesucht wurde, blühte London in der farbenfrohen Popkultur. Miyake machte sich an seinen freien Wochenenden auf zur Londoner King's Road. »Durch die 68er Revolution habe ich erkannt, woran ich glaube und den Wert dieser

les mannequins, le vêtement. Grâce à eux aussi, la mode devient un langage.

Mais au Japon, dans les années 50, le dessin de mode n'est pas considéré comme un choix d'étude convenant aux garçons. Dès son adolescence, pourtant, Miyake se passionne pour les revues de mode. En 1959, il s'inscrit aux cours de graphisme de la prestigieuse Tama Art University de Tokyo. Le dessin de mode ne faisant pas l'objet d'un programme séparé, Miyake doit, racontera-t-il plus tard, affronter un barrage psychologique, «car la mode était le domaine réservé des femmes. Etait-il envisageable que je pusse m'y infiltrer? De plus, la mode, c'était Paris et les collections parisiennes. Je voulais sortir de ce carcan».

En 1960, à l'occasion d'une conférence internationale sur le design organisée à Kyoto, Miyake commence à révolutionner le monde du stylisme: comme le dessin de mode n'est pas au programme, il se plaint ouvertement de cette lacune aux organisateurs: il est fermement décidé à donner au croquis de mode ses lettres de noblesse. De grandes corporations, la Toray et Shiseido, lui confient ses premières commandes alors qu'il est encore étudiant. Avant même d'obtenir ses diplômes en 1964, il produit un spectacle intitulé *A Poem of Cloth and Stone* (1963). Cette représentation a pour objet de montrer que le vêtement peut être tout à la fois création visuelle et «outil» purement utilitaire: «Par le biais du vêtement, nous voulons éveiller l'imagination. Bien que les modèles s'inspirent du style contemporain, il ne s'agit pas vraiment d'un défilé de mode. Je pense que le stade suivant sera l'avènement du vêtement tourné vers l'avenir. J'ai mis beaucoup de robes longues dans mon spectacle, non pas en tant que tenues de soirée mais simplement pour leur forme. J'aimerais que cet évènement marque la naissance de l'habillement visuel au Japon.»[2] En amont de ce plaidoyer pour le «vêtement visuel» de demain, sa volonté de distanciation vis-à-vis de la haute couture est explicite. Pourtant, avant de pouvoir innover réellement, il lui faut poser les bases de sa doctrine.

Miyake arrive à Paris en 1965 pour etudier à l'Ecole de la Chambre Syndicale de la Couture Parisienne. La même année il entre comme apprenti chez Guy Laroche. Son irruption dans le monde très sélect de la haute couture intervient à une époque troublée qui débouchera finalement sur les émeutes de mai 1968. «Mes premières années à Paris ont été très importantes car elles ont servi de tremplin à ma carrière; les notions de ‹beauté› et d'‹esthétique› du corps humain restaient trop rigides pour moi. Heureusement, les perceptions se trouvaient bousculées par le vent de liberté qui soufflait en 1968. Les solennels ‹Chère Madame›, les ‹je vous en prie› me parurent tout à coup complètement dépassés. Les gens descendaient dans la rue, je ne pensais qu'à me joindre à eux. J'ai quitté mon emploi, j'ai traîné quelques mois, mais comme je

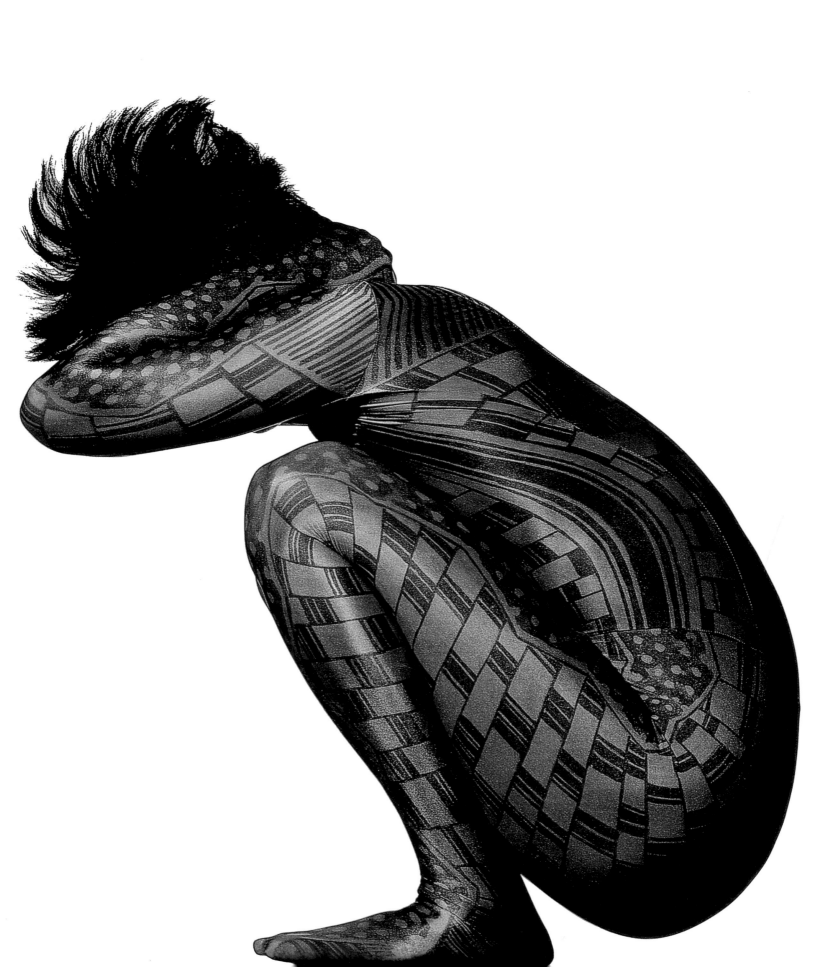

Miyake soon attracted commissions at home. The Shiseido corporation asked him to create designs for corporate clothing for the Expo, and the Toray corporation invited him to participate in a fashion show called *The Knit Exhibit*. He responded to the invitation in a futurist spirit by designing modular ready-to-wear garments that the wearers could assemble in the combinations of their choice. This invention for the age of the new, confident Japan, he called "Constructible Fashion".

"The importance of the time and the people cannot be underestimated," said Miyake. "The Expo was a time of social energy and national pride. 1970 was a special year and I realized I had to start something new." He talked to many textile factories and designers and realized the potential for work in Japan. Much was expected of him because he had worked abroad. He could contribute to creating original Japanese design by staying in the country at exactly the moment the nation was re-establishing its direction.

The Miyake Design Studio opened in Tokyo in April 1970 with the help of Tomoko Komuru, who became his longstanding business partner. It was a collaborative enterprise. Makiko Minagawa, the textile designer, joined Miyake from the start, together with a close group of friends who have remained affiliated to the studio ever since. Miyake was thirty-one years old; the apprenticeship was over and he was ready to begin his career. Two basic concepts were subsequently applied to the ethos of the studio. After the experience of America as a great cultural mix, Miyake was impressed by the ideal of freedom which was implied in the American dream. Freedom was to become the studio catchword, especially when exploring the relationship between clothing and the human body. Secondly, Miyake had to invent designs which were as "democratic" and comfortable as jeans and t-shirts.

At the end of 1970, Miyake's first collection was presented to Diana Vreeland at *Vogue*. In this first year he used a print design based on tattoos, which were closely associated with the downtown *yakuza* gangsters. Incorporated into the patterns were the faces of Janis Joplin and Jimi Hendrix, both recently departed. This East-West motif was worn close to the body as the "second skin". In his search for an equivalent to jeans, Miyake turned to *sashiko* quilting which had been used in Japan since the Nara period in the eighth century. This tough cloth for working garments and *kendo* and *judo* outfits was softened and adapted for industrial manufacture, and it formed a perfect material for coats. Miyake also needed to discover a fabric that could be applied universally to women of all shapes and sizes and which could be aimed at Sixties Western and Japanese markets. Polyester jersey, cut in squares and geometrical forms, was the ideal. One of Miyake's first zoomorphic garments was a flowing,

Grundsätze schätzen gelernt. Zuvor konnte man sich nur für bestimmte Personen und Dinge begeistern. Ich stellte diese Exklusivität in Frage. Die französische Kultur erschien mir schwerfällig und kopflastig. Dagegen liebte ich die Lebendigkeit Londons und konnte mich mit seiner Ausstrahlung identifizieren. Das gab mir das Selbstvertrauen, den Weg weiterzugehen, den ich von Anfang an für den richtigen gehalten hatte. Ich sammelte Kraft, um in der Zukunft einen Traum zu verwirklichen.«

Auch Miyakes Begeisterung für Amerika dauerte in Paris an. Die Neue Welt war der Ursprung einer großartigen Popkultur, die sich ihm aus einer französischen Perspektive erschloß. In Paris lernte er die Arbeiten von Robert Rauschenberg, Claes Oldenburg und Jasper Johns kennen. 1968 reiste er mit der Absicht nach New York, sich für immer in Amerika niederzulassen. Nach dem Sound der Beatles, behauptete er, reize ihn nun die Intensität von Jimi Hendrix und Janis Joplin — die rauchig-leidenschaftliche Stimme Amerikas.

Nach sechs Monaten in dem New Yorker Studio von Geoffrey Beene kehrte Miyake im Winter 1969/70 kurz nach Japan zurück. Er traf dort auf ein Japan, das sich inmitten einer enormen Umwälzung befand. 1970 war das Jahr der Weltausstellung in Osaka. Die wirtschaftliche Weltachse hatte sich verschoben. Trotz fehlender natürlicher Ressourcen hatte Japan sich zu einer wichtigen Industriemacht entwickelt. Zu dem wirtschaftlichen Aufschwung kam ein neues Gefühl kultureller Selbstsicherheit. Dem Land waren enorme gesellschaftliche Opfer abverlangt worden, und nun drängte sich die verschüttete Frage nach der wahren Identität Japans wieder in den Vordergrund. Statt der vorherrschenden Amerikanisierung während der Okkupation bestand jetzt die Möglichkeit zu einer eigenständigen japanischen Kultur, die einheimische Traditionen mit westlichen Strömungen in neuer, moderner Weise verbindet. Auf der Weltausstellung in Osaka hatte Tadanori Yokoo für Japan einen Pavillon aus Stoff geschaffen. Das Gebäude war von einem scharlachroten Gerüst umgeben, auf dem lebensgroße Schaufensterpuppen als Bauarbeiter gekleidet neben schwarzen Krähen hockten. Das Modell zeigte die Nation im Wiederaufbau, unter den Blicken der Symbole ihrer Vergangenheit. Miyake erhielt sehr schnell Aufträge in Japan. Shiseido beauftragte ihn, Hostessen-Uniformen für die Weltausstellung zu entwerfen, und Toray lud ihn ein, an einer Modenschau mit dem Titel *The Knit Exhibit* teilzunehmen. Seine Antwort auf diese Einladung war futuristisch inspiriert: Er kreierte modulare »ready-to-wear«-Kleidungsstücke, die von den Trägern nach eigenen Wünschen kombiniert werden konnten. Diese Erfindung für das neue, selbstbewußte Japan nannte er »Mode zum Zusammensetzen«. »Man darf die Bedeutung dieses Zeitpunktes und der Menschen nicht unterschätzen«, sagte Miyake. »Die

n'avais pas terminé ma formation de base, je suis
entré chez Givenchy à qui je dois beaucoup et où j'ai
été très heureux.» Alors que Paris défile dans les rues,
Londres s'affirme comme la capitale exubérante et flo-
rissante de la culture pop. Miyake y passe souvent le
week-end. King's Road est son lieu de prédilection.
«Les évènements de 68 m'ont aidé à voir clair en moi-
même et à m'affirmer. Jusque-là, je ne me passionnais
que pour certaines personnes et pour certaines
choses. J'ai remis en question ce côté exclusif. La culture française me semblait pesante et trop intellec-
tuelle. A l'inverse, j'aimais la turbulence de Londres et
je me suis tout de suite senti à l'aise dans l'atmo-
sphère de cette ville. Ensuite, je me suis mis à croire
en moi-même et j'ai trouvé ma voie, trouvé la force de
concrétiser ma vision de l'avenir.»

Handkerchief Dress, 1970
Photo: Tenmei Kano

Même à Paris, l'Amérique continue d'exercer une
certaine fascination sur Miyake. Le Nouveau Monde
est alors le temple d'une formidable culture populaire
qu'il perçoit par le biais de la culture française. A Paris,
il découvre le travail de Robert Rauschenberg, Claes
Oldenburg et Jasper Johns. En 1969, il part pour New-
York, bien décidé à s'installer définitivement aux Etats-
Unis. Après les chansons des Beatles, il avait besoin,
dit-il, de la violence d'un Jimi Hendrix ou d'une Janis
Joplin dont la voix éraillée fait frémir toute l'Amérique.

Après une période de six mois dans l'atelier new-
yorkais de Geoffrey Beene, Miyake retourne quelque
temps au Japon, durant l'hiver 1969—1970. Il retrouve
un pays en pleine mutation. En 1970 a lieu l'exposition
d'Osaka. L'axe économique mondial vient d'être boule-
versé. Malgré son manque de ressources naturelles, le
Japon est devenu une grande puissance industrielle.
Le redressement économique s'accompagne d'un
regain de confiance en matière culturelle. Mais le pays
a fait un énorme sacrifice social et la nature de l'identité japonaise reste encore mal définie. Le phénomène
d'américanisation qui a dominé pendant toute la
période de l'occupation se trouve dès lors remplacé
par une culture japonaise indépendante, assimilant traditions ancestrales, influences occidentales et une
toute nouvelle modernité. Lors de l'exposition d'Osaka,
Tadanori Yokoo, chargé de réaliser le pavillon du textile
japonais, conçoit un bâtiment enrobé d'échafaudages
d'un rouge écarlate sur lesquels des maçons factices
travaillent sous le regard de corbeaux noirs, symbole
d'une nation dont la reconstruction a lieu sous la protection de symboles ancestraux.

Miyake obtient bientôt diverses commandes dans
son propre pays. Shiseido le charge de concevoir les
uniformes de ses employés pour l'exposition, et la
société Toray lui demande de participer à un défilé de
mode, *The Knit Exhibit.* Dans un esprit futuriste, il dessine alors des tenues de prêt-à-porter modulables que
le client peut combiner et marier selon ses goûts ou
son humeur. Ce principe parfaitement moderne, à

Top:
Hikeshi, 1970
Photo: Kishin Shinoyama

Bottom:
Unit Cloth, 1969
Photo: Kishin Shinoyama

Constructible Cloth, 1969
Photo: Kishin Shinoyama

Page 34/35 · Seite 34/35
Sashiko
Spring/Summer 1971
Photo: Hideko Yoshikawa for
Mainichi Newspapers

35

pointed "bat cape" from 1970. In this first year the Miyake Design Studio had found a fabric for a world market, had reinvented a traditional Japanese fabric, and had introduced the Miyake concept of clothing as a "second skin".

Miyake's collections in the early Seventies often emphasized rural Japanese roots using check designs from farmers' cloth and cotton crepe made from dipping the cloth in the cold waters of northern Japan. Like the *sashiko* quilting, traditional farmers' style encouraged practicality and durability and was contrary to the conventional refinement of the fashion world. One of the first Miyake photo-shoots took place early in the morning at Ueno Station in Tokyo with the models standing among the farm women who were bringing the vegetables in from the country. Miyake respected these hard-working women. He was a provincial boy from Hiroshima who had gone north to the great city of Tokyo and he identified with these country women. Miyake's concept of industry extended from factory mass-production to the physical labour of the fields, and especially to the surviving craftsmanship of Japan. Beside these elements of native tradition, Miyake imported exotic checks from Bali and with the Toray Corporation he developed an acrylic knit, Pewlon, for flowing lines and billowing capes. Irish wool was used for coats that might have been worn by travellers of some back road of Edo Japan. He exploited traditional cloth while also experimenting with new fabric inventions. He borrowed internationally while reasserting the qualities of his own culture.

Years later Miyake avoided the label "Japanese designer". He disapproved of the categorisation of Japanese designers as if they were a common entity. The success of the Miyake Design Studio in the Seventies did create a climate for Japanese design in general to become a prevalent force internationally. His collections were shown not only in Tokyo, but at an early stage he showed the collections in New York and Paris, where he had established press offices.

Miyake's internationalism freely transcended his strong Japanese identity. He was very impressed by Leni Riefenstahl's photographs of the Nuba of the Sudan. In 1976, he created part of his collection in homage to the Nuba imagery, using brilliantly striped Pewlon. The Nuba physiques were to be sensational material for public posters when a Riefenstahl exhibition was held in Tokyo in 1980. The exhibition was designed by Eiko Ishioka, who, like Miyake, found the colour, pattern and vitality a contrast to the black and white imagery of suffering Africa.

Miyake's early collaborations included work with Tadanori Yokoo, the graphic designer Miyake called "the Hokusai of our time". Yokoo had established a style of poster design which owed as much to *ukiyo-e* woodblock tradition as it did to psychedelic culture.

Weltausstellung setzte eine Welle gesellschaftlicher Energien und nationalen Stolzes frei. 1970 war ein ganz besonderes Jahr, und mir wurde klar, daß ich etwas Neues beginnen mußte.« Er sprach mit zahlreichen Textilfabrikanten und Modemachern und lotete das Potential für seine weitere Arbeit in Japan aus. Man setzte große Hoffnungen auf Miyake, da er im Ausland gearbeitet hatte. Zu einem Zeitpunkt, da die Nation sich neu orientierte, könnte er dazu beitragen, ein eigenständiges japanisches Design zu gestalten. Das Miyake Design Studio wurde mit Hilfe von Tomoko Komuru, seinem langjährigen Geschäftspartner, im April 1970 in Tokio eröffnet. Es war ein Gemeinschaftsunternehmen: Der Textildesigner Makiko Minagawa war von Anfang an dabei, ebenso eine kleine Gruppe von Freunden, die seither mit dem Studio in engem Kontakt stehen. Miyake war einunddreißig Jahre alt. Er hatte seine Lehrjahre abgeschlossen; seine Karriere konnte beginnen. Zwei Grundideen bestimmten die Philosophie des Studios. Nachdem Miyake Amerika als Mischung der Kulturen erfahren hatte, war er beeindruckt von dem Freiheitsideal, das der amerikanische Traum implizierte. Freiheit wurde zum Leitgedanken für sein Studio, besonders wenn es darum ging, die Beziehung zwischen Kleidung und Körper zu ergründen. Außerdem ging es Miyake darum, Kleidung zu kreieren, die so »demokratisch« und bequem war wie Jeans und T-Shirt.

Ende 1970 präsentierte Miyake seine Kollektion Diana Vreeland von der Zeitschrift *Vogue*. In diesem ersten Jahr entwarf er ein Druckmuster, das den Tätowierungen der Yakuza-Gangster, der japanischen Mafia, nachempfunden war. In die Muster integriert waren die Gesichter von Jimi Hendrix und Janis Joplin, die beide kurz zuvor gestorben waren. Das Ost und West verbindende Stoffdessin wurde eng am Körper anliegend getragen, wie eine »zweite Haut«. Auf seiner Suche nach einem passenden Äquivalent für Jeansstoff stieß er auf *Sashiko*-Steppstoff. Dieser traditionelle, mit geometrischen Mustern abgesteppte Stoff wurde seit der Nara-Periode im achten Jahrhundert in Japan gefertigt. Den festen, fast steifen Stoff, der für Arbeitskleidung sowie für die Anzüge beim *kendo*, der japanischen Fechtkunst, und beim *judo* genommen wurde, verfeinerte er so, daß er sich für die industrielle Fertigung eignete. Als Mantelstoff war er ideal. Miyake suchte außerdem nach einem Material, das für Frauen jeder Größe und Figur geeignet war und sich sowohl in Japan als auch im Westen vermarkten ließ. Polyesterjersey, in Rechtecke und geometrische Formen geschnitten, entsprach genau seinen Vorstellungen. Eines der ersten von Miyake nach der Natur geformten Stücke war ein fließendes, zugespitztes »Fledermaus-Cape« aus dem Jahre 1970. In diesem ersten Jahr war es dem Miyake Design Studio gelungen, einen Stoff für den Weltmarkt zu fabrizieren, ein tradi-

l'image de l'optimisme ambiant, il le nomme *«mode à construire»*. «On ne peut sous-estimer l'importance du temps et des hommes», explique le créateur. «L'exposition a eu lieu pendant une période de dynamisme social et d'orgueil national. 1970 a été une année particulière. Je sentais qu'il était temps pour moi de me lancer sur de nouvelles voies.»

S'adressant à de nombreux stylistes et industriels du textile, Miyake prend conscience qu'un formidable potentiel de travail s'offre à lui au Japon. Parce qu'il connaît déjà le marché étranger, on attend beaucoup de lui. En restant au Japon, il pourrait largement contribuer à la naissance de la haute couture japonaise, au moment même où le pays s'apprête à se lancer dans de nouvelles directions.

En avril 1970, à trente et un ans, Miyake a fini sa période d'apprentissage, il se sent prêt: encouragé par un groupe de fidèles amis et collaborateurs, il ouvre donc le Miyake Design Studio à Tokyo, avec l'aide de Tomoko Komuru, qui allait devenir son fidèle partenaire commercial.

La dessinatrice de textiles Makiko Minagawa est là dés le début. A sa suite, divers créateurs — toujours présents aujourd'hui — participent eux aussi à la naissance de la maison. Miyake entend y développer deux principes de base: tout d'abord une grande ouverture d'esprit, à la manière du rêve américain, un climat de liberté propice au travail de réflexion sur la relation entre le vêtement et le corps. Ensuite, une créativité «démocratique», c'est-à-dire la conception de tenues aussi confortables que le jean ou le T-shirt.

A la fin de l'année 1970, la première collection de Miyake est présentée à Diana Vreeland de *Vogue*. On y découvre un imprimé inspiré des tatouages chers aux gangsters *Yakuza* (qui sévissent dans les bas-quartiers des grandes villes japonaises). Mariés aux divers motifs, les visages de Janis Joplin et de Jimi Hendrix, tous deux récemment disparus. Les modèles, où se mélangent l'Orient et l'Occident, se portent près du corps, comme autant de «secondes peaux». Le jean façon Miyake est conçu à partir de *sashiko* (tissu ouaté et piqué, à motifs géométriques et couleurs primaires), utilisé au Japon depuis la période Nara (VIIIe siècle). A priori grossière, cette étoffe qui sert habituellement pour les vêtements de travail et les tenues de *judo* ou de *kendo* (escrime), adoucie, adaptée pour une fabrication industrielle se révèle un formidable tissu pour manteaux. Miyake, qui a également voulu mettre au point un matériau universel pouvant satisfaire toutes les femmes quelles que soient leur taille et leur morphologie, propose un jersey de polyester coupé en diverses formes géométriques. C'est ainsi que, dès 1970, l'un des premiers vêtements «zoomorphes» voit le jour: il s'agit d'une cape «chauve-souris» ondoyante. Il n'aura donc suffi que d'une seule année au Miyake Design Studio pour concevoir une

Sashiko
Worn by Fusae Ichikawa
Autumn/Winter 1973
Photo: Kishin Shinoyama for
Asahi Graph

ISSEY *with* K

974年1月29日、30日 ISSEY ゆ KANSAI SHOW が、次の各位の御協力によって実現

式会社一琳 一村産業株式会社 株式会社イッセイミヤケインターナショナル エイテル株式会社 オールスタイル株式会社 カワボウテキスタイル株式会社 社 キング商事株式会社 株式会社 造型堂 シルバーシャツ早稲株式会社 株式会

KANSAI
PHOTO: KISHIN SHINOYAMA

西武百貨店·西武百貨店商事部·株式会社·高島屋·大染工業株式会社·東レ株式会社·日本オリベッティー株式会社·株式会社 フェニックス·丸紅株式会社·ロンシャン株式会社·株式会社 ワコール

Issey with Kansai poster, 1974
Photo: Kishin Shinoyama

Yokoo's lusciously coloured print designs of paradise scenes with reference to Milton's *Paradise Lost* were applied to Miyake fabrics in the mid-Seventies. Indian Tantric symbols, which fascinated Yokoo, then decorated Miyake silk dresses of voluminous proportions, which billowed like sails.

Using this diverse range of fabrics, both new and traditional, the Miyake Design Studio emphasized simplicity of form. The simplification led ultimately to a garment created in essence from a single piece of cloth in a simple square to which sleeves were added. The design for such a coat in 1976 was called *A Piece of Cloth* and it was produced in a striped knit of cotton and linen. This minimalist garment was clearly derived from the kimono tradition rather than Western couture. The art of allowing the cloth to flow over the body contrasts with the idea of construction or assembly of the garment on the body. These distinctions between simplification or reduction and construction distinguish many Oriental and Western traditions. The simplicity of Japanese aesthetics, from the fifteenth century painting of Sesshu or the seventeenth century architecture of Katsura was much admired by the pioneers of Western modernism. Miyake could develop a tradition which was neither Eastern nor Western, or in Miyake's own phrase, where "East Meets West". When the simplification was complete, as in *A Piece of Cloth*, the effect was both classical and timeless. "I always try to get all my answers by returning to one piece of cloth, the most basic form of clothing", claimed Miyake.

In Japan, Miyake's reputation was growing from show to show as he challenged all concepts of catwalk couture. He created a sensation in Tokyo when he paraded his models from top to bottom of an eight-storey car park at the Seibu department store in Shibuya in 1971. With Eiko Ishioka he staged *The Issey Miyake Show* at the Shibuya Parco in 1975, followed the next year by *Issey Miyake and Twelve Black Girls*, a challenge to any concept of an exclusively Oriental style. The exuberance of Miyake's *Twelve Black Girls*, including a snarling Grace Jones, was in perfect accord with the Parco image. This sense of design provided a window on world culture, with a modern look embracing ethnic beauty. The look was full of colour and movement in the midst of a society which was stultifyingly monochrome in its conformist pursuit of the economic dream.

Fly with Issey Miyake, the show held at the Meiji Jingu Indoor Field in Tokyo in 1977 was greeted by Aromu Mushiake, an enthusiastic writer in *Sports Nippon*, as a profound evocation of human vitality. "On the stage, a long white cross-shaped runway, appeared the models, two or three at a time, starting at a walk side by side and then gradually breaking into a dance. Immediately, everyone in the audience clapped their hands to the rhythm. The show started

tionelles japanisches Gewebe neu zu beleben und die Idee von Kleidung als »zweiter Haut« zu etablieren.

Miyakes Kollektionen aus den frühen Siebzigern bezogen sich oft auf die bäuerliche Kultur Japans: Verwendet wurden kariertes Bauernleinen oder Baumwollkrepp, hergestellt, indem der Stoff in die kalten Gewässer von Japans Norden getaucht wurde. Wie der *Sashiko*-Steppstoff unterstrich auch der traditionelle bäuerliche Stil den Aspekt der Tragbarkeit und Haltbarkeit der Kleidung und bildete einen Gegensatz zu der üblichen Raffinesse der Haute Couture. Eine der ersten Foto-Serien von Miyake-Kreationen fand dann auch im Morgengrauen am Ueno-Bahnhof in Tokio statt; die Mannequins standen inmitten der Bauersfrauen, die das Gemüse vom Land auf den Markt brachten. Miyake hatte vor den schwer arbeitenden Bauersfrauen große Achtung. Da er aus dem provinziellen Hiroshima stammte und sich von dort nach Norden in die Metropole Tokio aufgemacht hatte, konnte er sich mit den Frauen vom Land identifizieren. Miyakes Auffassung von Industrie umfaßte die Massenproduktion in den Fabriken ebenso wie die körperliche Arbeit auf den Feldern, besonders aber die überlebende Handwerkskunst Japans. Neben diesen Elementen einheimischer Tradition importierte Miyake exotische Karos aus Bali, und gemeinsam mit der Toray Corporation entwickelte ein Acrylgewebe, Pewlon, für fliessende Linien und schwingende Capes. Irische Wolle wurde für Mäntel verwendet, die sogar Reisende aus der längst vergangenen Edo-Epoche hätten tragen können. Miyake verwendete traditionelle Stoffe ebenso, wie er mit neuen Materialien experimentierte. Er zitierte internationale Stile und behauptete gleichzeitig die Besonderheiten seiner eigenen Kultur. Jahre später vermied Miyake es, als »japanischer Designer« etikettiert zu werden. Er hielt nichts von einer Kategorisierung, die den Eindruck erweckte, daß die japanischen Designer eine Einheit bildeten. Dennoch kann man sagen, daß der Erfolg des Miyake Design Studios in den Siebzigern dem japanischen Design allgemein zu einer breiteren internationalen Anerkennung verhalf. Miyakes Kollektionen wurden nicht nur in Tokio gezeigt, sondern bereits sehr früh in New York und Paris, wo er Pressebüros eingerichtet hatte.

Miyakes Internationalität ermöglichte es ihm, seine ausgeprägte japanische Identität hinter sich zu lassen. Sehr beeindruckt war er von Leni Riefenstahls Fotografien der Nuba im Sudan. Als Hommage an die Bilderwelt der Nuba kreierte er 1976 einen Teil seiner Kollektion in leuchtend gestreiftem Pewlon. Die Körper der Nuba waren Vorlage für eine aufsehenerregende Plakatserie anläßlich einer Leni Riefenstahl-Ausstellung in Tokio 1980. Die Ausstellung war von Eiko Ishioka konzipiert worden, die, wie Miyake, Farben, Muster und Lebendigkeit als Kontrast zum Schwarzweißbild des leidenden Afrika empfand.

étoffe adaptée au marché mondial, réinventer un tissu traditionnel japonais et lancer le concept de vêtement «seconde peau».

A l'époque, les collections de Miyake reprennent souvent des thèmes ruraux japonais; il utilise beaucoup les motifs à carreaux inspirés des tissus campagnards ainsi que du crêpe de coton obtenu en plongeant les étoffes dans les eaux glacées du nord du pays. Tout comme le *sashiko*, ce style traditionnel paysan se veut pratique et durable, très éloigné du style raffiné qu'impose la mode conventionnelle.

L'une des premières séances de photos de Miyake a lieu tôt le matin à la gare Ueno de Tokyo. Des mannequins se tiennent parmi des paysannes venues vendre leurs légumes à la ville. Miyake, le petit provincial d'Hiroshima, a toujours éprouvé un immense respect pour ces femmes de la terre qui lui rappellent ses origines. Pour lui, les valeurs de son pays reposent aussi bien sur les ouvriers qui travaillent aux chaînes de montage que sur les paysans peinant aux champs ou encore et surtout sur les derniers petits artisans du Japon.

En plus de ces motifs traditionnels, Miyake importe des quadrillés exotiques de Bali et développe en collaboration avec la Toray Corporation une toile de maille acrylique: le Pewlon. Il aime particulièrement sa fluidité qui convient parfaitement à ses grandes capes voltigeantes. Il utilise de la laine d'Irlande pour ses manteaux qui rappellent ceux que portaient les voyageurs de la lointaine époque Edo. Il se sert d'étoffes anciennes qu'il n'hésite pas à marier aux dernières inovations textiles. Il puise dans la tradition internationale tout en préservant les valeurs de sa propre culture.

Miyake refusera toujours d'être catalogué «styliste japonais». Il n'accepte pas que l'on enferme tous les créateurs japonais dans une seule et même catégorie, qu'on en fasse une seule et même entité. Le succès du Miyake Design Studio et de ses collections non seulement montrées à Tokyo mais aussi exportées à New York et Paris où le créateur ouvre des bureaux de presse quasiment dès le début, crée surtout un nouveau climat qui permet au style japonais, en général, de s'imposer sur le plan international.

Le génie d'Issey Miyake transcende donc largement sa forte identité japonaise. En 1976, très impressionné par les photos de Leni Riefenstahl sur les Nubiens du Soudan, le créateur consacre une partie de sa collection à l'imagerie populaire de ce peuple, utilisant pour l'occasion un Pewlon à rayures hautement chamarré. Mais ce n'est qu'en 1980 que l'extraordinaire photogénie des Nubiens sera révélée au grand public par le biais d'une exposition d'œuvres de Riefenstahl mise en scène à Tokyo par Eiko Ishioka, grande directrice artistique de l'époque: pour valoriser encore les photos en noir et blanc d'une Afrique douloureuse, elle joue les contrastes à la manière de Miyake, mariant les affiches à des couleurs et formes pleines de vitalité.

Marilyn Monroe
Spring/Summer 1970
Photo: Bishin Jumonji for *an an*

Page 40/41 · Seite 40/41
Hocho Cut
Spring/Summer 1976
Photo: Tatsuo Masubuchi
(Studio 77 Tokyo)

with a group of strong but delicate colours as one sees in Morocco; green, white, earth tones and indigo. As the show progressed, the colours became more vital. By visually illustrating human movements, body-lines and muscle tones, the show evoked a sense of the ever-present life-force."[3] By 1982 Miyake's extravaganza had culminated in a show on the decks of the aircraft carrier *U.S.S. Intrepid*, bathed in pink light as it lay moored on the Hudson River. Miyake had appropriated a New York landmark as a further platform for his propagation of internationalism.

Throughout the first decade of the Miyake Design Studio, the position between Eastern and Western traditions was a preoccupation which had to be qualified frequently. "Western clothing is already perfect," said Miyake later. "I realized that, even if I tried, there is not much I could do to improve it. On the other hand, the Japanese kimono is a tradition frozen in time. It does not belong to contemporary life. My challenge as a clothing designer has been to create something different, not traditionally Japanese, not purely Western, but something which has the best of both: a new genre of clothing."[4] His lack of a Western background he regarded as an advantage.

Issey Miyake East Meets West, a summary of Miyake's work up to 1977, was published in 1978. Though designed in a large format by Ikko Tanaka, and beautifully printed, the book was bound in softcovers as a statement of position rather than a luxurious showcase of design. The title itself provided a conceptual base from which Miyake could develop without boundaries. It was a logical conclusion to "flying" with Issey Miyake into a new period where the old divisions no longer applied. The studio existed like a laboratory in Tokyo. The European platform for the collections was by then well established in Paris. The sources of inspiration were worldwide.

"*East Meets West* existed as words which expressed the possibility of indefinite, eternal human qualities. The title created a framework for my work, and functioned as a means to remove boundaries and reveal myself as a creator. It was not intended to be more than a small window through which to observe my work." Having removed the boundaries, Miyake was to return to his declared universal theme of the relationship between the body and cloth.

Reading the texts in Miyake's book *Issey Miyake Bodyworks* (1983), one is impressed not only by the diversity of the commentators, from artists, designers, philosophers, sociologists and models to Miyake himself, but by the recurring statements of freedom that his clothes encourage. The freedom may have come from the "masks" which one commentator believed the clothes provided in the same manner as body decoration might determine the confidence and the role of the Nuba warrior. In addition to the psychological free-

Zu Miyakes frühen Gemeinschaftsproduktionen zählte die Zusammenarbeit mit dem Graphikdesigner Tadanori Yokoo, den Miyake in Erinnerung an den berühmten Holzschnittmeister des frühen 19. Jahrhunderts »den Hokusai unserer Zeit« nannte. Yokoo hatte Plakate kreiert, deren Stil der *Ukiyo-e*-Tradition, der japanischen Kunst des Holzschnitts, wie der psychedelischen Popkultur gleichermaßen verpflichtet war. Yokoos knallbunte Druckentwürfe stellten Szenen aus dem Paradies dar, in Anspielung auf Miltons *Verlorenes Paradies*. Mitte der Siebziger wurden diese Szenen auf Miyake-Stoffe gedruckt. Indische Tantra-Symbole, von denen Yokoo fasziniert war, schmückten nun Miyakes üppig bauschende Seidenkleider, die wie Segel im Wind wehten.

Bei dieser Vielfalt an neuen und traditionellen Materialien und Mustern betonte das Miyake Design Studio die Schlichtheit der Form. Die Vereinfachung führte letztlich zu einem Bekleidungsstück, das lediglich aus einem Stück Stoff — ein einfaches Rechteck, an das Ärmel angesetzt waren — gefertigt wurde. Ein solches Mantelmodell, *A Piece of Cloth* genannt, wurde 1976 aus einem Baumwoll-Leinengewebe hergestellt. Als Vorbild für dieses minimalistische Modell erkannte man deutlich die Tradition des Kimono, nicht die westliche Mode. Die Kunst, dem Stoff die Möglichkeit zu geben, den Körper zu umfließen, steht im Gegensatz zur westlichen Tradition des Konstruierens und Zusammensetzens von Kleidung. Dieser Unterschied zwischen Vereinfachung bzw. Reduktion auf der einen und Konstruktion auf der anderen Seite trennt in vielen Fällen die östliche von der westlichen Tradition. Die Schlichtheit japanischer Ästhetik, wie sie sich in den Bildern des berühmten Landschaftsmalers Sesshu aus dem 15. Jahrhundert oder der Gartenarchitektur von Katsura aus dem 17. Jahrhundert ausdrückt, fand bei den Vorreitern der westlichen Moderne große Bewunderung. Miyake gelang es, eine Tradition zu schaffen, die weder rein östlich noch rein westlich geprägt war, sondern in der, mit Miyakes Worten, »der Osten den Westen trifft«. Das Ergebnis dieser Vereinfachung hinterließ, wie bei dem Modell *A Piece of Cloth*, einen klassischen und zeitlosen Eindruck. »Ich versuche immer, zu diesem einen Stück Stoff zurückzukehren, weil es die elementare Form der Bekleidung ist«, erklärte Miyake.

Miyakes Ansehen wuchs von Schau zu Schau, indem er sämtliche Vorstellungen von Laufstegmode in Frage stellte. In Tokio wurde 1971 seine Modenschau zur Sensation, als er die Mannequins durch alle acht Stockwerke im Parkhaus des Seibu Kaufhauses im Stadtteil Shibuya marschieren ließ. Gemeinsam mit Eiko Ishioka produzierte er 1975 die *Issey Miyake Show* im Shibuya Parco. Im darauffolgenden Jahr lieferte die Schau *Issey Miyake and Twelve Black Girls* eine Absage an die Vorstellung von einem ausschließ-

Tadanori Yokoo, graphiste que Miyake surnomme le «Hokusai de notre temps» (Hokusai était un grand maître de l'Ecole *Ukiyo-e*, 1760–1849), collabore à ses premières collections. Pour ses posters, Yokoo a innové dans un style particulier, à la fois fortement influencé par la tradition de la gravure sur bois, par le thème de *l'ukiyo-e* (images d'un monde flottant) et par la culture psychédélique. Aux alentours de 1975, Miyake se sert de ses imprimés aux couleurs chatoyantes, évoquant le *Paradis Perdu* de Milton. Et pour ses volumineuses robes de soie qui se meuvent à la manière de voiles au vent, Miyake emprunte encore à Yokoo les symboles tantriques indiens qui fascinent tant le dessinateur.

Ainsi, utilisant plusieurs types d'étoffes, alliant tradition et avant-garde, le Miyake Design Studio tend de plus en plus à simplifier la forme.

Cette épuration de la ligne finit par déboucher sur un vêtement créé, pour l'essentiel, à partir d'un seul carré de tissu auquel il suffit d'ajouter des manches. En 1976, ce type de manteau *A Piece of Cloth* est fait de tricot de coton et de lin rayé. Par son aspect minimaliste, il émane davantage de la tradition du kimono que de la haute couture occidentale, la volonté de laisser l'étoffe «ruisseler» sur le corps contrastant avec la rigueur de construction ou d'ajustage propre au vêtement occidental.

C'est à cette différence précisément que l'on distingue le plus souvent la tradition venue de l'Est de la tradition issue de l'Ouest, beaucoup plus structurée. La simplicité de l'esthétique japonaise, illustrée par les tableaux de Sesshu (célèbre paysagiste du XVe siècle) ou par l'architecture Katsura du XVIIe a toujours fait l'admiration des adeptes du modernisme occidental. Fort de cette constatation, Miyake développe un style qui est, selon ses propres termes, «la rencontre de l'Est et de l'Ouest». Une fois la simplification poussée à son extrême, comme avec le fameux *A Piece of Cloth*, il obtient un effet tout à la fois classique et intemporel. «J'essaie toujours de revenir à un unique morceau de tissu, au plus ‹fondamental›» explique le créateur.

Au Japon, la renommée de Miyake grandit de collection en collection, même s'il bouleverse tous les poncifs qui gouvernent la haute couture. En 1971, il fait sensation à Tokyo lorsqu'à Shibuya il choisit, en guise de podium pour son défilé, les huit étages du parking du grand magasin Seibu. En 1975, le couturier réalise avec la collaboration d'Eiko Ishioka le *Issey Miyake Show* au Parco de Shibuya, puis, l'année suivante, le spectacle *Issey Miyake and Twelve Black Girls* bouscule totalement le concept d'un style exclusivement oriental.

L'exubérance des *Twelve Black Girls*, où l'on découvre une Grace Jones au sourire menaçant, enflamme la presse Japonaise dès l'instant où les

Issey Miyake and Twelve Black Girls poster
Spring/Summer 1976
Photo: Hajime Sawatari

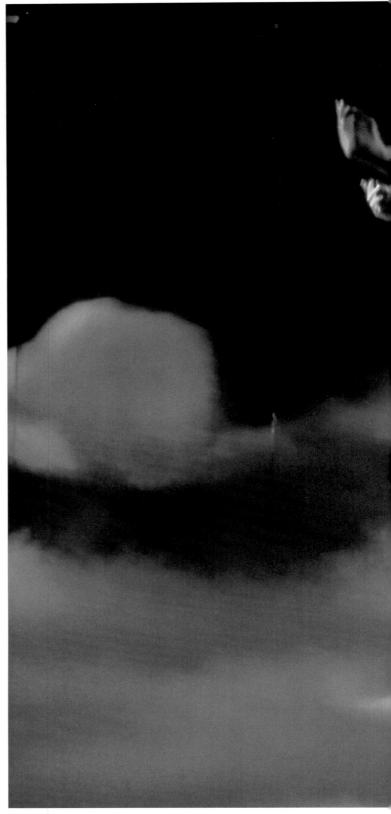

Page 46/47 · Seite 46/47
Issey Miyake and Twelve
Black Girls
Spring/Summer 1976
Photo: Noriaki Yokosuka

Page 48/49 · Seite 48/49
*Issey Miyake and Twelve
Black Girls*
Spring/Summer 1976
Jessica Brown, Barbara Jackson,
Grace Jones, Ester Kamatari,
June Murphy, Jan Maden, Denis
Paschál, Ramona Saunders,
Toukie Smith, Carol Standifer,
Barbara Summers, Karen Wilson
Photo: Noriaki Yokosuka for
Eiko by Eiko

Issey Miyake Show pamphlet
Shohana Cotton Jumpsuit
Spring/Summer 1974
Photo: Noriaki Yokosuka

dom came the freedom of the body at ease with its movement, or of the body unharnessed in its "second skin".

By the early Eighties, Miyake was able to separate his design into two quite distinct directions. There was the research into new and sometimes spectacular territory with wide-ranging experiments with fabrics. Secondly, there was the desire for practicality. By the start of the decade everyday clothing had become much more stylized. Changes in working and business clothes had become acceptable internationally. Miyake wanted to develop both the fantastic element and the practical. He established *Plantation* in 1981 as what he called "clothes for real life". They were elegant, functional and relatively inexpensive. Plantation used natural fibres, a straight cut with a sturdy top stitch and a comfortable looseness around the sleeves. These were "living clothes" designed for action with pronounced simplicity.

In early 1982, debate around Miyake left the fashion pages as he laid down a trail of signs for semiotic analysis in the art world. His design appeared on the cover of *Artforum*, edited by Ingrid Sischy, and was the subject of the magazine's editorial. The subject was Miyake's wide-shouldered bamboo and rattan bodice, as delicate as the lacquer armour of a medieval warrior. It veiled the model's bare breasts, but was as much a token of release as constraint. "Issey Miyake's jacket is a paraphrase of light samurai armour," the editorial astutely observed. "It is also a metaphor for a certain relationship to nature. The outfit is a contemporary skin – its bodice is both cage and armour, lure and foil. The artificial shoulders of the "iron butterfly" evoke the assertiveness and weaponry of pioneer-woman-space invader. Eastern and Western, a picture of fashion – she's a legend."[5]

The *Bodyworks* project took the idea of the "second skin", which Miyake had followed since his first tattoo garments, into a science fiction world. Miyake's "second skin" was then literally represented in a solid, moulded breast plate. The installations for the project involved suspending identical silicon mannequins from the ceilings of galleries in Tokyo, San Francisco, Los Angeles and London against stark, minimal settings. Though the bamboo and rattan armour echoed tradition, the repetition of these suspended figures pointed to a cyborg generation encased in silent march through space.

Past and future, East and West, body and cloth – the poles of Miyake's creativity – were all combined in 1988, the year of his fiftieth birthday. Using the title *A-ŪN*, Miyake installed his most ambitious exhibition at the Musée des Arts Décoratifs in Paris. The title referred to a point of silent balance or unspoken communication. To that extent it suggested a unity, however Zen its connotation, between the old divisions

lich fernöstlichen Stil. Die Exaltiertheit von Miyakes *Twelve Black Girls*, zu denen auch eine zähnefletschende Grace Jones gehörte, war bereits von dem Moment an, als die extravaganten Mannequins am Tokioter Haneda Flughafen ankamen, ein Schock für die japanische Presse. Miyake durchbrach die Barrieren eines insulären und konformen Japan, indem er einer Nation, die nur mit der Verwirklichung ökonomischer Träume beschäftigt war, einen Einblick in eine globale Kultur bot.

1977 fand die Schau *Fly with Issey Miyake* im Meiji Jingu Indoor Field in Tokio statt. Begeistert wurde sie von Aromu Mushiake, der für *Sports Nippon* schrieb, als eine fundamentale Visualisierung menschlicher Vitalität kommentiert: »Auf einem langen, kreuzförmigen Laufsteg erschienen immer zwei oder drei Mannequins gleichzeitig; zuerst nebeneinander gehend, begannen sie allmählich zu tanzen. Sofort klatschte das Publikum den Rhythmus mit. Die ersten Modelle beeindruckten durch kräftige, dennoch subtile Farben, wie man sie aus Marokko kennt: Grün, Weiß, erdige Töne und Indigo. Mit der Zeit wurden die Farben lebendiger. Die Bewegungen des Körpers, seine Linien und Muskelstränge wurden visuell umgesetzt. Die Schau versinnbildlichte damit die Idee der allgegenwärtigen Lebenskraft.«[3]

1982 kulminierte Miyakes extravaganter Präsentationsstil in einer Modenschau auf dem Deck des Flugzeugträgers *U.S.S. Intrepid*. Verankert am Hudson River, war das Schiff in pinkfarbenes Scheinwerferlicht getaucht. Miyake hatte so ein Wahrzeichen von New York zum Laufsteg seiner Botschaft der Internationalität gemacht.

In der ersten Dekade des Miyake Design Studios wurde die eigene Stellung zwischen östlicher und westlicher Tradition immer wieder neu definiert. »Westliche Kleidung ist bereits perfekt«, erklärte Miyake später. »Ich erkannte, daß, selbst wenn ich es versuchen würde, mir nicht mehr viel zu verbessern übrig bliebe. Demgegenüber steht der japanische Kimono als eine zeitlose Tradition. Er gehört nicht zu unserem heutigen Leben. Meine Herausforderung als Kleidungsdesigner bestand darin, etwas anderes zu entwerfen, das weder traditionell japanisch noch ausschließlich westlich ist und das Beste von beiden vereint: ein neues Genre von Kleidung.«[4] Daß er keinen westlichen Hintergrund hatte, bewertete er als einen Vorteil, der ihm Freiheit ließ.

1978 erschien Miyakes Buch *Issey Miyake East Meets West*, eine Zusammenstellung seines Schaffens bis zum Jahr 1977. Ikko Tanaka hatte das großformatige Werk konzipiert, das auf edlem Papier gedruckt, aber nur in einen broschierten Umschlag gebunden war: Es sollte Miyakes Positionen und Ideen darstellen und kein luxuriöser Bildband seiner Kunst sein. Allein der Titel lieferte eine konzeptionelle

mannequins débarquent avec éclat à l'aéroport de Tokyo. Le nouveau «look», jaillissant au sein d'une société obsédée par la poursuite d'un terne rêve économique, est révolutionnaire. Il déborde de couleurs et de mouvement.

En 1977, le spectacle du Meiji Jingu Indoor Field de Tokyo, *Fly with Issey Miyake*, est salué avec enthousiasme par Aromu Mushiake, collaborateur de la revue *Sport Nippon*. C'est, de son point de vue, une évocation profonde de la vitalité humaine: «La scène représentait une longue piste d'atterrissage toute blanche, en forme de croix. Les mannequins sont apparues par petits groupes de deux ou trois, marchant d'abord côte à côte. Puis, petit à petit, elles se sont mises à danser. Immédiatement, les spectateurs ont commencé à taper dans leurs mains pour marquer le tempo. Au début, les couleurs, quoique fortes, étaient délicates et évoquaient des paysages marocains, des verts, des blancs, des tons de terre, d'indigo. Mais au fur et à mesure, les nuances sont devenues plus toniques. En illustrant ainsi les mouvements du corps humain, les lignes de la silhouette, la souplesse des muscles, le spectacle donnait une impression omniprésente de vitalité.»[3] En 1982, Miyake donne libre cours à son imagination et à sa fantaisie; il organise un défilé sur le pont du porte-avion américain *U.S.S. Intrepid* amarré le long de la Hudson River, baignée d'une lumière rose. En s'appropriant un véritable «monument» new-yorkais, Miyake entend proclamer son internationalisme.

Pendant ses dix premières années d'existence, le Miyake Design Studio se préoccupe avant tout d'imposer son image: une savante union de traditions orientales et occidentales. Le créateur s'explique souvent sur ce sujet: «Le vêtement occidental a atteint la perfection; je sais bien que, même si j'essayais, je ne pourrais pas y apporter beaucoup d'améliorations. Par contre, le kimono japonais est resté figé dans le temps et n'appartient pas à l'époque contemporaine. C'est pourquoi je me suis fixé pour mission, en tant que styliste, de créer quelque chose de différent, qui ne soit ni classiquement japonais, ni purement occidental, mais plutôt un produit qui emprunte le meilleur de ces deux univers au profit d'un nouveau concept vestimentaire.»[4] Pour Miyake, ne posséder aucune racine occidentale apparaît comme une liberté en plus.

Le livre *Issey Miyake East Meets West*, qui est publié en 1978, résume toute l'œuvre du créateur jusqu'en 1977. Bien que conçu en grand format par Ikko Tanaka et luxueusement imprimé, l'ouvrage sort en version brochée: en effet, pour Miyake, ce livre doit être plus une déclaration de foi qu'une somptueuse anthologie de ses créations. D'emblée, le titre établit une base conceptuelle à partir de laquelle Miyake extrapole librement. Suite logique au fameux «Fly with», l'ouvrage entraîne le lecteur vers un nouvel espace où toutes les vieilles divisions perdent leur

Page 52/53 · Seite 52/53
Fly with Issey Miyake
Autumn/Winter 1977/78
Photo: Sachiko Kuru

Spinnaker
Print Design by Tadanori Yokoo
Autumn/Winter 1977/78
Photo: Noriaki Yokosuka

Page 55 · Seite 55
Paradise Lost
Print Design by Tadanori Yokoo
Spring/Summer 1977
Photo: Noriaki Yokosuka

Page 56/57 · Seite 56/57
Waterfall Body
Autumn/Winter 1984/85
Photo: Art Kane for *Stern*

that separated East and West. *A-ŪN* appears like the punctuation in Miyake's career, after which the themes of his work were fully defined and his language or medium was established, whatever changes in his vocabulary or fabric might later develop. The clothes were displayed in the exhibition on mannequins of thin wire. They suggested threads of human structure like cables within the machinery of the body. The designs were becoming increasingly biomorphic. A coat of traditional oiled paper cocooned the body as if in amber crystal. The textures of a woollen coat looked like a forest seen from the air. Images flowed with associations to rocks, shells, the insect world, the barks of trees or the trail of seaweed. This was a poetic language. The freedom he had vehemently established with the founding of the Miyake Design Studio allowed him to invent at will according to his inspiration. There was no restriction. "There are no boundaries for what can be fabric, for what clothes can be made from. Anything can be clothing."[6] Since his student period of fascination with American magazines, Miyake had greatly admired the photographs of Irving Penn, who, in addition to being a great portraitist and fashion photographer, was the unparalleled master of the still-life. The *A-ŪN* exhibition coincided with the publication of a book of Penn's photographs of Miyake's design. The clothes had been sent to the photographer's New York studio, where he had heightened the sense of their shape, colour and quality by photographing them against a pure white background. Both Penn and Miyake shared a common feeling for simplification. The geometry of the clothes and the subtleties of density or transluscence of the fabric were free from superfluous detail save for the hair and face of the model. Suspended in white space, the clothes formed perfect, abstract objects. The Penn photographs became part of an ongoing series of posters with minimal typography and design by Ikko Tanaka. Tanaka's design with Miyake, as with the book *Issey Miyake East Meets West*, combined traditional formality with clean modernity. Miyake's design could not be further refined as still-life. The equivalent representation of the work in motion had yet to be explored.

Diana Vreeland, writing in *Issey Miyake East Meets West*, described her first visit in 1977 to Miyake's boutique at the Place du Marché-Saint-Honoré in Paris. "The boutique was closed, but Issey's whole corner was of glass and inside was the prettiest and most unusual sight: as one looked in, one saw only bleached wood, stairs and platforms, everything blond and light, with latticed railings reminiscent of the Heian Period scrolls and paintings and the beautiful centuries-old city of Nara. There, right in the heart of Paris was a gleaming, happy, sunny corner filled with green and fruit-bearing trees."[7] The Miyake store existed as the oasis of harmony in the chaos of the city, just as the classic Japanese interior offered order

Grundlage, von der aus Miyake sich grenzenlos weiterentwickeln konnte. Es war die logische Konsequenz des »Fliegens« mit Issey Miyake in eine neue Zeit, in der die früheren Trennungslinien keine Rolle mehr spielten. Das Studio in Tokio avancierte zum Laboratorium. Die europäische Bühne für seine Kollektionen war fest in Paris etabliert. Die Quellen seiner Inspiration kamen aus der ganzen Welt.

»*East Meets West*: diese Worte drücken die Möglichkeit unerschöpflicher Kreativität aus. Der Titel schuf den Rahmen für meine Arbeit, war dazu angelegt, Grenzen zu überwinden und mich selbst als Künstler zu offenbaren. Er war wie ein kleines Fenster, durch das man meine Arbeit betrachten konnte.« Nachdem er die Grenzen überwunden hatte, sollte Miyake sich wieder seinem erklärten Hauptthema, der Beziehung zwischen Körper und Stoff, zuwenden.

Liest man in Miyakes nächstem Buch *Issey Miyake Bodyworks* (1983), ist man sowohl beeindruckt von der Vielfalt der Äußerungen zu Miyakes Arbeiten — Künstler, Designer, Philosophen, Soziologen, Mannequins sowie Miyake selbst kommen zu Wort — als auch davon, daß sich die Äußerungen immer wieder auf das Erlebnis von Freiheit in Miyakes Kleidung beziehen. Einer der Autoren meinte, die Befreiung läge in der »Maskierung« durch die Kleidung, ähnlich wie die Körperbemalung der Nubakrieger deren Identität und Selbstvertrauen fördert. Neben der seelischen Freiheit kommt die Freiheit des Körpers im Einklang mit seinen Bewegungen sowie die Leichtigkeit dieser »zweiten Haut« zum Ausdruck. Ab den frühen Achtzigern gelang es Miyake, sein Design in zwei unterschiedliche Richtungen weiterzuentwickeln. Auf der einen Seite stieß er bei großangelegten Experimenten mit neuen Materialien in unbekannte und oft aufregende Gebiete vor. Auf der anderen Seite stand die Suche nach tragbarer Kleidung. Seit Beginn des Jahrzehnts bekam auch die Alltagskleidung mehr Stil. Veränderungen in der Business-Mode hatten sich international durchgesetzt. Miyake wollte sowohl das phantasievolle als auch das praktische Element weiterentwickeln. 1981 entwarf er *Plantation*, »Kleidung für das wirkliche Leben«, wie er sich ausdrückte. Die Kleider waren elegant, funktional und relativ preisgünstig. Die Serie *Plantation* zeichnete sich durch natürliche Materialien sowie gerade Schnitte mit betonten Absteppungen und bequemen weiten Ärmeln aus. Es war Kleidung von betonter Einfachheit, in der man »leben« konnte. 1982 spielte sich die Beschäftigung mit Miyakes Stil nicht mehr nur auf den Modeseiten ab: Die Zeichen, die er prägte, wurden in der Kunstwelt semiotisch analysiert. Ein Modell von ihm erschien auf dem Umschlag von *Artforum*, herausgegeben von Ingrid Sischy, und wurde im Editorial des Magazins besprochen. Es war Miyakes breitschultriges Oberteil aus Bambus und Rattan, das so fein gearbeitet war wie die lackierte

sens: le studio de Tokyo fait office de laboratoire. Paris est sa plate-forme européenne, la vitrine de ses collections. Le monde est la source de son inspiration. «Avec *East Meets West,* je voulais rappeller l'existence de qualités humaines infinies, éternelles. Le titre m'a servi de cadre de travail; il m'a aidé à faire tomber certaines barrières et à me révéler en tant que créateur. Mais il ne se voulait aussi qu'une petite fenêtre par laquelle on pourrait observer mon travail.» Miyake revient à son thème universel favori: la relation entre le corps et le tissu.

En découvrant les textes publiés dans son livre *Issey Miyake Bodyworks* (1983), on ne peut qu'être impressionné par le nombre et la diversité des commentateurs qui s'y expriment, qu'il s'agisse d'artistes, de stylistes, de philosophes, de sociologues, de mannequins ou de Miyake lui-même. La notion de liberté est l'un des thèmes vedette de l'ouvrage: les vêtements, selon un commentateur, dissimulant le corps derrière un «masque» l'incitent à se libérer, à la manière des peintures-maquillages qui, tracées sur le corps des guerriers nubiens, leur insufflent courage et confiance. Après la liberté mentale vient la liberté physique, le bien-être d'un corps libre de ses mouvements, à l'aise dans sa «seconde peau».

Au début des années 80, Miyake se lance dans deux directions bien distinctes: d'un côté, il part à la recherche de terrains vierges et, pour satisfaire son goût du spectaculaire, continue à travailler sur de nouvelles matières. D'un autre côté, il veut faire du «pratique». Les vêtements de tous les jours sont devenus beaucoup plus stylisés. Les changements apportés aux tenues de travail sont acceptés partout dans le monde. Miyake veut développer à la fois le fantastique et l'ordinaire. En 1981, avec sa ligne *Plantation*, il crée ce qu'il nomme le «vêtement à vivre», une gamme élégante, fonctionnelle et relativement bon marché caractérisée par des fibres naturelles, des coupes droites surpiquées et toujours d'amples emmanchures. Il s'agit là de vêtements «vivants», actifs, rigoureusement simples.

Début 1982, l'image d'Issey Miyake n'est plus confinée à l'univers de la mode. Les nombreux symboles que drainent ses créations donnent lieu à diverses analyses sémiotiques dans le monde des arts. Le modèle qu'il crée alors paraît en couverture du magazine *Artforum,* dont la rédactrice est Ingrid Sischy, et l'éditorial lui est consacré. Il s'agit d'un bustier aux larges épaulettes fait de bambou et de rotin, raffiné à la manière des armures de laque des guerriers médiévaux. Ce corselet qui voile les seins est signe d'affranchissement autant que d'esclavage. «Ce modèle fait penser à l'armure délicate d'un samouraï» observe avec justesse l'éditorialiste. «C'est également la métaphore d'un certain rapport à la nature. Cette tenue serait comme la peau de notre temps — à la fois cage

Issey Miyake Spectacle
Bodyworks Exhibition
1983, Tokyo
Photo: Yoshikuni Kawashima

Page 60 left/a gauche
Seite 60 links
Issey Miyake Spectacle
Bodyworks Exhibition
1983, Tokyo
Photo: Yoshikumi Kawashima

Page 60 right/a droite
Seite 60 rechts
Issey Miyake Spectacle
Bodyworks Exhibition
1983, San Francisco
Photo: Fujitsuka Mitsumasa

Page 61 · Seite 61
Issey Miyake Spectacle
Bodyworks Exhibition
1985, London

59

Issey Miyake Spectacle
Bodyworks Exhibition
1983, Tokyo
Photo: Yoshikuni Kawashima

Page 62· Seite 62
Issey Miyake Bodyworks
Fashion without Taboos Exhibition/
Boilerhouse Project
1985, London

Issey Miyake Spectacle
Bodyworks Exhibition
1983, San Francisco
Photo: Fujitsuka Mitsumasa

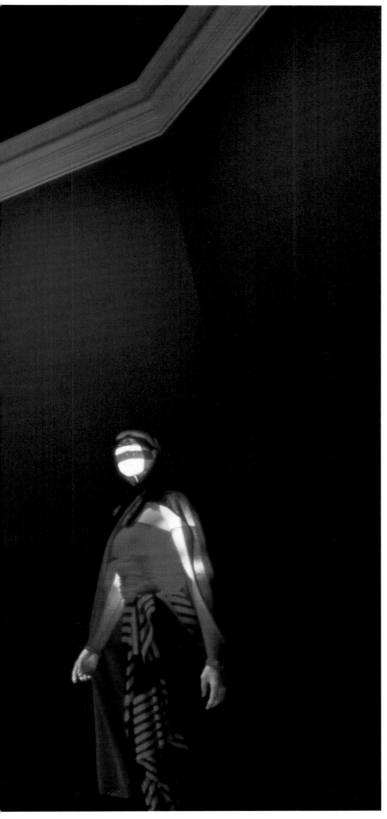

Page 66 · Seite 66
Issey Miyake Bodyworks
Fashion without Taboos Exhibition/
Boilerhouse Project
1985, London

Page 67 · Seite 67
Issey Miyake Spectacle
Bodyworks Exhibition
1983, Tokyo
Photo: Yoshikuni Kawashima

Issey Miyake Spectacle
Bodyworks Exhibition
1983, Tokyo
Photo: Yoshikuni Kawashima

65

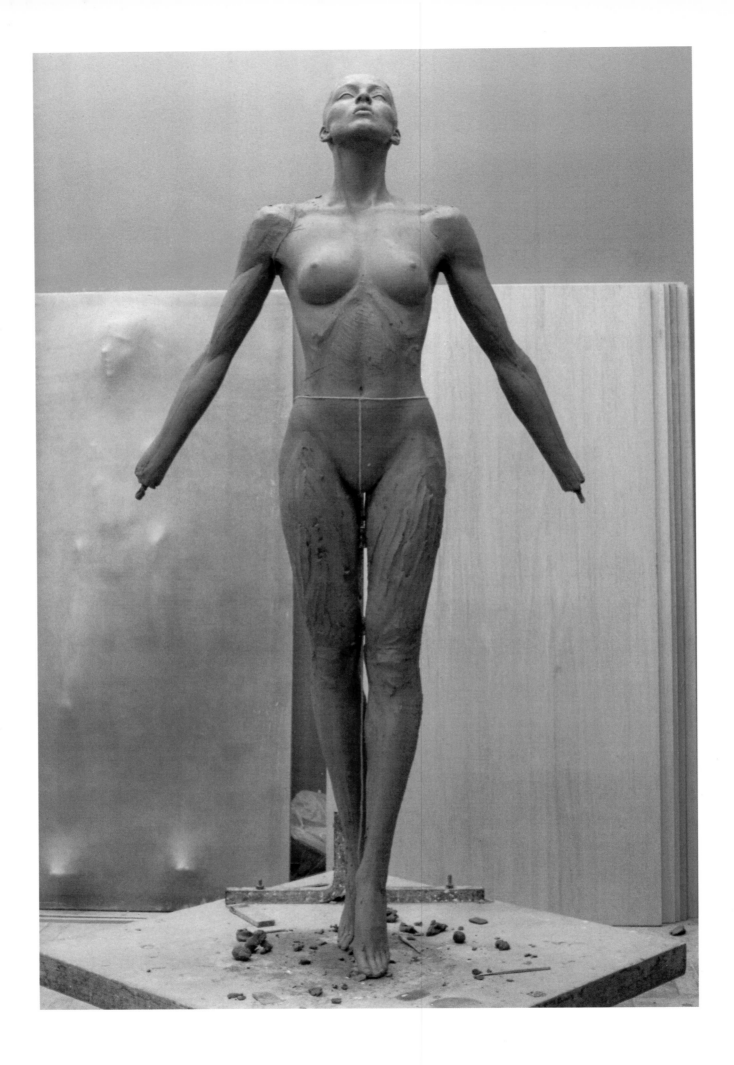

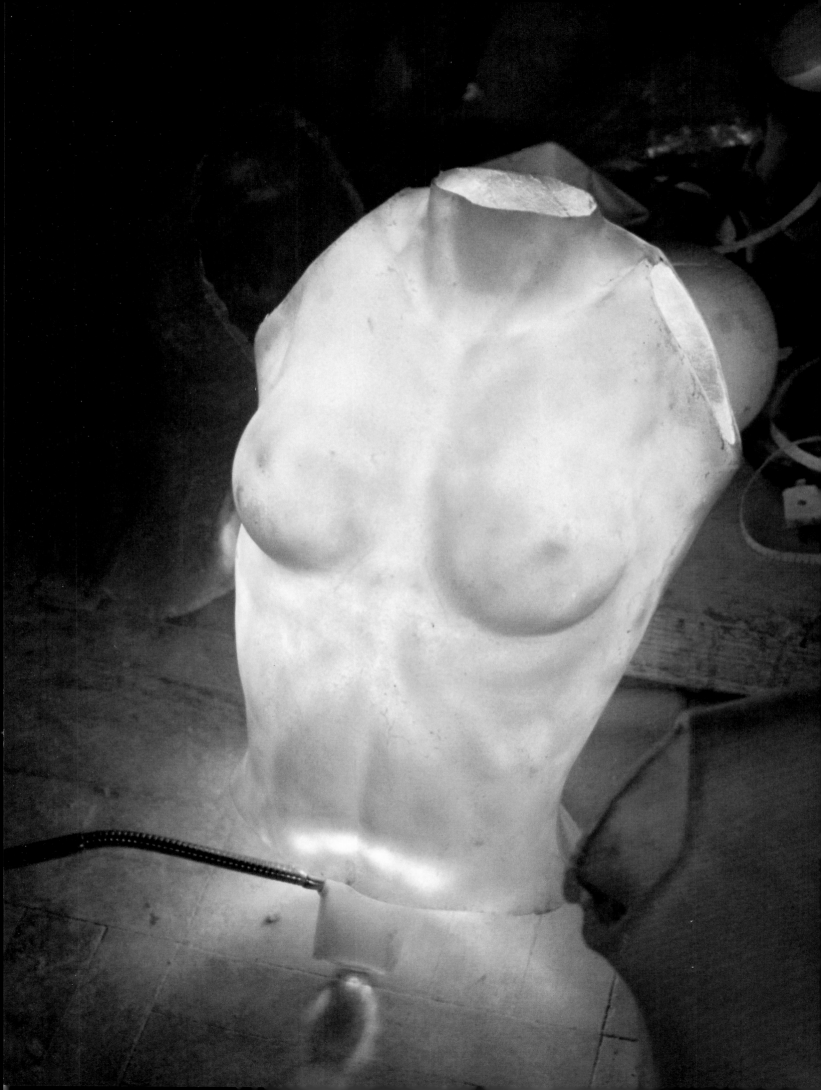

Plastic Body
Worn by Lisa Lyon
Autumn/Winter 1980/81
Photo: Robert Mapplethorpe

Page 73 · Seite 73
Rattan Body
Spring/Summer 1982
Photo: Tsutomu Wakatsuki

Page 74/75 · Seite 74/75
Issey Miyake A-ŪN Exhibition
1988, Paris
Photo: © S. Anzai

Page 76/77 · Seite 76/77
Issey Miyake A-ŪN Exhibition
1988, Paris
Photo: © S. Anzai

Shell Knit Coat
Spring/Summer 1985
Photo: Gilles Tapie

in contrast to exterior disarray. Since the establishment of the Tokyo flagship boutique in 1976, Miyake has engaged the late Shiro Kuramata on the design of the stores. From the beginning Kuramata was a vital partner in the presentation of Miyake's design. Kuramata was one of the most influential of modern Japanese designers, he worked with the Memphis group in Milan in the Eighties. His design of the current men's store in Tokyo involves the hanging of the clothes on giant steel cables in metallic contrast to the Heian associations described by Vreeland. Miyake's public image for his shop window, as with the Penn posters, highlights his vision with a simplicity as dramatic as his museum installations.

The spirit of collaboration enables Miyake to maintain his public presence. "The worst thing about the 1980s is that designers became stars. Design is not an extension of my ego. Design is teamwork. I employ many people. Design carries great responsibility."[8] When he came to the launch of his fragrance *L'Eau d'Issey* in 1992, Miyake created a distinctive tapering bottle, topped by a spherical stopper. The packaging of the perfume was then designed in collaboration with Fabien Baron, the New York designer. Detail in packaging was as important as the shop window itself.

Throughout the Eighties, Issey Miyake not only sustained the activities of the studio but also broadened his role as a cultural entrepreneur within Japan. After seeing the ceramics of Lucy Rie, a Viennese refugee in London, he regarded her work as more "Japanese" than the tea bowls from his own culture, which were weighted with the associations of their long history.

Her work was installed on water in an exhibition designed by the architect Tadao Ando at the Sogetsu Kaikan, the heart of Japanese traditional aesthetics in Tokyo in 1987 at Miyake's instigation. The following year he collaborated with Eiko Ishioka and Shiro Kuramata on a staging and projection of Marcel L'Herbier's long-lost classic silent film *L'Inhumaine* of 1923 at the Bunkamura Orchard Hall in Tokyo. Beyond his role as a designer Miyake served as a vital cultural bridge, dissolving barriers and championing causes from ceramics to cinema.

The exhibition *Issey Miyake A-ŪN* resulted in a complete re-assessment of direction. Attendance at the exhibition in Paris was large. The book of Penn's photographs highlighted Miyake's spectacular designs. The installation of the show was marvellous, but Miyake knew he had "big audiences to look, but small audiences to wear". Once again he had to concentrate on moving from the spectacular to lighter, practical clothing.

The year of *A-ŪN*, 1988, was the year Miyake began work on the major theme of pleats. As early as 1975 he had explored pleats in white linen crepe. The poly-

Rüstung eines japanischen Kriegers des Mittelalters. Es ließ die Brust des Mannequins durchschimmern und war gleichermaßen Symbol für Freiheit und Zwang. »Issey Miyakes Jacke ist die Paraphrase einer leichten Samurai-Rüstung«, so der treffende Kommentar der Herausgeberin. »Ebenso ist sie eine Metapher für eine besondere Beziehung zur Natur. Das Outfit ist eine zeitgenössische Haut — das Oberteil ist Käfig und Harnisch in einem, Werkzeug der Verführung und Schutzobjekt zugleich. Die künstlichen Schultern des ›eisernen Schmetterlings‹ versinnbildlichen die Selbstsicherheit und Wehrhaftigkeit einer Pionierfrau, einer Weltraum-Kriegerin. Ost und West, ein Bild der Mode — sie ist eine Legende.«[5] Das Bodyworks-Projekt versetzte die Idee der »zweiten Haut«, die Miyake seit seinen ersten Tätowierungsmodellen verfolgt hatte, in eine Science-Fiction-Welt. Miyakes »zweite Haut« war ein massiv geformtes Brustschild. Das Projekt wurde in Galerien von Tokio, San Francisco, Los Angeles und London installiert. In kahlen, minimalistisch gestalteten Räumen schwebten identische Schaufensterpuppen von den Decken. Obwohl die Rüstung aus Bambus und Rattan Tradition ausstrahlte, verwies die Wiederholung dieser herabhängenden Figuren auf eine Cyborg-Generation, festgehalten auf ihrem schweigenden Marsch durch das Weltall.

Vergangenheit und Zukunft, Ost und West, Körper und Stoff — die Pole von Miyakes Kreativität verschmelzen im Jahre 1988, dem Jahr seines fünfzigsten Geburtstags. Unter dem Titel Issey Miyake A-ŪN installierte Miyake seine ambitionierteste Ausstellung im Musée des Arts Décoratifs in Paris. Der Titel bezog sich auf einen Moment stillen Einvernehmens beziehungsweise wortloser Kommunikation. So sehr das an Zen-Buddhismus erinnern mochte, verwies der Titel auf eine Einheit der beiden altbekannten Pole Ost und West. Die Kleider wurden in der Ausstellung an Puppen aus dünnem Drahtgeflecht präsentiert. Die Drähte erinnerten an die Adern und Sehnen des menschlichen Körpers, sie glichen Kabeln im Innern der Körpermaschinerie. Miyakes Entwürfe nahmen zunehmend biomorphe Formen an. Ein Mantel aus klassischem Ölpapier umhüllte den Körper wie ein Kokon aus bernsteinfarbenem Kristall. Die Struktur eines wollenen Mantels erinnerte an einen Wald, betrachtet aus der Vogelperspektive. Die Bilder strömten über von Assoziationen mit Felsen, Muscheln, Insekten, Baumrinden oder schlingernden Algen. Es war eine poetischen Sprache. Die Freiheit, die Miyake mit der Gründung des Miyake·Design Studios energisch propagiert hatte, erlaubte es ihm, seiner Inspiration freien Lauf zu lassen — ohne Grenzen. »Es gibt keine Beschränkungen bei den Materialien, aus denen Kleidung gemacht sein kann. Alles kann Kleidung sein.«[6] A-ŪN bildete eine Art Höhepunkt in Miyakes Schaffen. Die Themen seines

et bouclier, outil de séduction et objet de protection. Les épaules artificielles de ce ‹papillon de fer› évoquent la force et l'aplomb d'une pionnière, d'une guerrière descendue de l'espace. Elle est l'Orient et l'Occident, elle est l'image même de la mode, elle est un être de légende.»[5]

Bodyworks fait de nombreuses fois référence à la notion de «seconde peau». Miyake y tient. Il lui est resté fidèle depuis ses premiers imprimés tatoués, il l'a introduite dans un univers de science-fiction. Cette «seconde peau» y devient une solide cuirasse moulée sur le corps. Et le créateur l'expose clairement par le biais de mannequins en plastique tous identiques suspendus au plafond de galeries de Tokyo, de San Francisco, de Los Angeles et de Londres, sur fond de décor austère et dépouillé. Tandis que bambou et rotin évoquent la tradition, ces légions de combattantes symbolisent une génération cybernétique engagée dans une marche silencieuse à travers l'espace.

Passé et futur, Orient et Occident, corps et toile — tous les grands thèmes chers à Miyake — atteignent leur apogée en 1988, l'année de ses cinquante ans. Miyake entre au Musée des Arts Décoratifs de Paris: c'est l'exposition Issey Miyake A-ŪN, ce qui signifie «point d'équilibre silencieux» ou encore «communication tacite». Ces termes font également référence à l'idée d'unité qui, même si elle rappelle la philosophie Zen, tire un trait sur les vieilles démarcations séparant l'Est de l'Ouest. A-ŪN apparaît comme un tournant dans la carrière de Miyake; dorénavant, ses thèmes sont parfaitement définis et son langage fermement établi, quels que soient les changements de vocabulaire ou de tissus qui apparaîtront plus tard. Les vêtements sont exposés sur des mannequins de fil de fer. Ces carcasses métalliques établissent un lien entre l'organisme humain et la machine. Les modèles deviennent de plus en plus biomorphes. Des pelisses en papier huilé traditionnel enveloppent les corps d'un cocon de cristal ambré. La texture d'un manteau de laine fait penser à une forêt vue d'avion. On découvre une longue suite d'images, d'associations d'idées entre roches, coquillages, insectes, écorces, arbres ou algues mouvantes. Une véritable poésie en mouvement. La liberté que Miyake a revendiquée en fondant le Miyake Design Studio lui permet d'inventer à loisir, de laisser voguer son imagination sans restriction. Pour lui «toute matière peut constituer une étoffe». Il s'arroge le droit «de fabriquer un vêtement à partir de n'importe quoi».[6]

Depuis la période où, jeune étudiant, il se plongeait avec fascination dans les magazines américains, Miyake admire les photos d'Irving Penn, non seulement excellent portraitiste et grand photographe de mode, mais encore maître incontesté de la nature morte. L'exposition A-ŪN coïncide avec la publication d'un recueil de modèles de Miyake photographiés par

Irving Penn Poster Exhibition
iii at ggg, 1988, Tokyo

Page 81 · Seite 81
Irving Penn Poster Exhibition
1992, Tokyo, Axis Gallery
Photo: Sasaki Studio Co, Ltd.

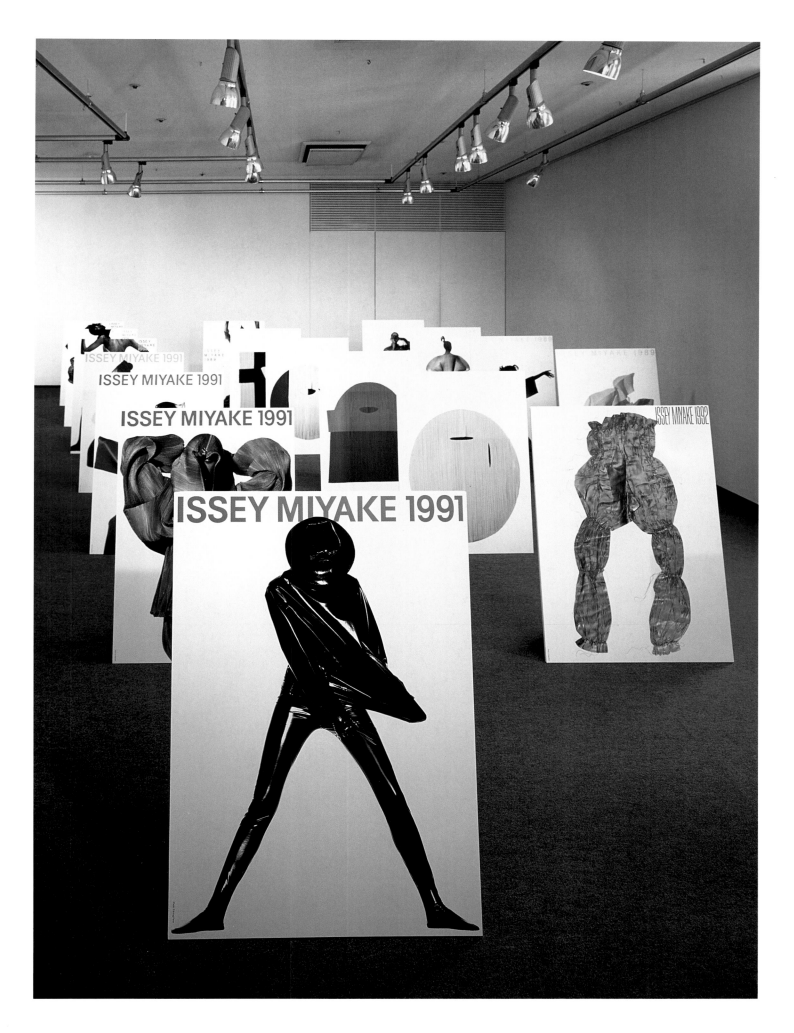

urethane coated jersey skirt worn with the famous rattan bodice on the front of *Artforum* in 1982 was pleated. Historically, the technique dates back to ancient Egypt. In modern times the reputation of the Venetian designer, Mariano Fortuny, was established at the turn of the century with pleats of the finest silk. For Miyake, pleats were the result of his search for the functional garment, as well as his fascination with the surface of the material. First he experimented with stretch fabrics and produced body-stockings decorated like the tattoos of his original "second skin" from the Seventies, but this application of the strech fabric had a limited market. He began to develop pleats first with woven cotton or polyester then with tricot jersey, so that the folds of the pleats were accompanied by the stretch of the jersey. The result was the establishment of the *Pleats Please* project in 1988 using polyester jersey in basic shapes and adding new colours and tones each year. *Pleats Please* represents Miyake's most simple design. Light and washable, the look was ideal for the modern age. *Pleats Please* is now marketed throughout the world. The subsequent modifications of the process have combined practicality with constant visual surprise.

"Pleats move and change form with the wearer's body movements. As the pleats move they change colours, giving an optical illusion like a kaleidoscope," he explained, "Pleats contain endless fascination for me and also inspire a multitude of images."9 Unlike the conventional method of pleating polyester with heat and then cutting the fabric to a design, Miyake reversed the process by designing the shape first and pleating the finished form.

The pleating press became the experimental focus as comparisons of different fabric compositions, including the use of wool, linen and cotton, were tested alongside variations in colour and tone of cloth. The initial graphic effect was of horizontal and vertical lines, but by turning the unpleated garment and feeding it into the pleating machines at an angle, diagonally pleated clothes were produced. As well as providing elasticity for the wearer, the pleats provided a constantly shifting play of light, heightening Miyake's sense of the surface of the cloth.

Miyake had hoped that children would enjoy the simple geometry of his *Pleats Please* exhibition at the Touko Museum of Contemporary Art in Tokyo in 1990. Following a similar installation he created for the exhibition *Energieën* at the Stedelijk Museum, Amsterdam earlier in the year, Miyake set pleated dresses in their abstract form, flat on the ground, recessed into the floor of the gallery. Visitors removed their shoes and walked around the ovals and rectangles of cloth in yellows, crimsons, ochres and black. At the Tokyo opening, guests arrived wearing these dresses and filling their flattened two-dimensional

Werkes waren damit definiert und seine Sprache und sein Medium voll entwickelt; mochten sich auch sein Vokabular und seine Materialien noch verändern.

Seitdem ihn als Student die amerikanischen Magazine fasziniert hatten, bewunderte Miyake die Fotografien Irving Penns. Penn war nicht nur ein großartiger Porträtist und Modefotograf, sondern auch ein unvergleichlicher Meister des Stillebens. Die Ausstellung *A-ÜN* fiel mit der Veröffentlichung eines Buches zusammen, in dem Irving Penn Modelle von Miyake fotografiert hatte. Die Kleider waren zu Penns Studio nach New York geschickt worden, wo er den Eindruck ihrer Form, Farbe und Qualität verstärkte, indem er sie gegen einen rein weißen Hintergrund ablichtete. Beiden, Penn und Miyake, war der Sinn für Vereinfachung gemein. Die Kleider waren in ihrer Geometrie und Subtilität der Dichte, beziehungsweise Durchsichtigkeit der Stoffe, von jedem überflüssigen Detail befreit, lediglich Haare und Kopf des Mannequins waren zu sehen. Im weißen Raum gleichsam schwebend, wurden die Kleider zu perfekten abstrakten Objekten. Penns Fotos bildeten die Grundlage einer Plakatserie mit minimaler typografischer Gestaltung von Ikko Tanaka. Tanakas Design für Miyake ebenso wie für sein Buch *Issey Miyake East Meets West*, verband traditionelle Formen mit modernem Purismus. Miyakes Design wurde so zum perfekten Stilleben. Die entsprechende Präsentation seiner Kreationen in bewegter Form stand noch aus.

In *Issey Miyake East Meets West* beschreibt Diana Vreeland ihren ersten Besuch in der Miyake Boutique am Place du Marché-Saint-Honoré in Paris im Jahre 1977: »Die Boutique war geschlossen, aber Isseys Laden hatte eine riesige Fensterfront, und innen tat sich einem der schönste und ungewöhnlichste Anblick auf: überall gebleichtes Holz; Treppen und Galerien, alles war hell und leicht gehalten, mit vergitterten Balustraden, die an Schriftrollen und Malereien aus der Heian-Periode, einer Zeit höfischer Eleganz und Verfeinerung, erinnerten und an die wunderschöne, Jahrhunderte alte Stadt Nara. Dort, mitten im Herzen von Paris, befand sich ein leuchtendes, fröhliches und sonniges Fleckchen, das mit grünen und früchtetragenden Bäumen geschmückt war.«7 Der Laden von Miyake schuf eine Oase der Harmonie im Chaos der Großstadt, genau wie das klassische japanische Interieur einen Kontrast zur Unordnung der Außenwelt bildete. Seit der Eröffnung des Hauptsitzes im Jahre 1976, der Boutique in Tokio, hatte Miyake den in der Zwischenzeit verstorbenen Shiro Kuramata mit dem Design der Läden beauftragt. Von Anfang an war Kuramata ein prägender Partner in der Präsentation von Miyakes Design. Kuramata, der in den frühen Achtzigern mit der Gruppe Memphis in Mailand gearbeitet hatte, war einer der einflußreichsten Designer des modernen Japans. Im Herrengeschäft in Tokio

Page 83 · Seite 83
Cicada Pleats
Spring/Summer 1989
Photo: Albert Watson for British *Elle*

Page 84/85 · Seite 84/85
Mutant Pleats
Autumn/Winter 1989/90
Photo: Oliviero Toscani for *Stern*

Penn. Les vêtements sont envoyés au studio new-yor-kais du photographe qui fait honneur à leurs formes, leurs couleurs, leurs textures en les immortalisant sur un fond d'un blanc immaculé. Penn et Miyake parta-gent un même amour pour l'épure. Le photographe souligne la géométrie des vêtements et les subtilités de densité ou au contraire de transparence des matières en débarrassant la photo de tout détail superflu, en ne laissant voir que le visage et la cheve-lure de la femme qui les porte. Comme suspendus dans un espace vierge, les vêtements deviennent des objets abstraits aux lignes nettes et parfaites. Les photos de Penn sont déclinées en affiches enrichies d'une typographie minimaliste signée Ikko Tanaka. Comme déjà dans le livre *Issey Miyake East Meets West*, le travail de Tanaka est un mélange de forma-lisme traditionnel et de sobre modernité. Le style de Miyake, traité là en natures mortes, atteint les limites du raffinement. Mais il lui reste encore à explorer les nombreuses possibilités offertes par les jeux de mou-vements.

Dans un texte de *Issey Miyake East Meets West*, Diana Vreeland décrit sa première visite à la boutique Issey Miyake, Place du Marché-Saint-Honoré à Paris. C'était en 1977. «La boutique était fermée mais la façade étant entièrement en verre, j'ai pu regarder à l'intérieur et découvrir un spectacle aussi beau que saisissant. Beaucoup de bois blanchi, beaucoup d'escaliers et de plates-formes, un univers blond et clair, des balustrades en treillis rappelant les peintures et manuscrits de la période Heian et la merveilleuse cité ancestrale de Nara. Là, en plein cœur de Paris, on découvre un paradis de lumière, de bonheur et de soleil où poussent des arbres verts, chargés de fruits.»[7] Tout comme un classique intérieur japonais, havre de paix contrastant avec le tohu-bohu de la rue, le magasin de Miyake est une sorte d'oasis harmo-nieuse perdue dans le chaos de la grande ville. Depuis l'ouverture de sa boutique pilote en 1976, à Tokyo, Miyake a toujours confié la décoration intérieure de ses espaces à Shiro Kuramata, aujourd'hui disparu, qui savait si bien mettre en valeur ses créations. Kura-mata, l'un des décorateurs les plus influents du Japon contemporain, a travaillé avec le groupe milanais Memphis dans les années 80. Pour la boutique Hommes de Tokyo, il suspend les vêtements à des câbles d'acier géants, contrastant avec les références à la période Heian (795—1185) décrites par Vreeland. Qu'il s'agisse de ses vitrines ou de ses affiches sig-nées Penn, Miyake tient toujours le même discours: c'est avant tout de simplicité qu'il veut parler.

Son esprit d'équipe lui permet aussi de rester très présent auprès du public. «Il est regrettable que, dans les années 80, les créateurs soient devenus de véri-tables stars. Je ne conçois pas mon art comme un moyen de devenir une vedette. Le design, c'est avant

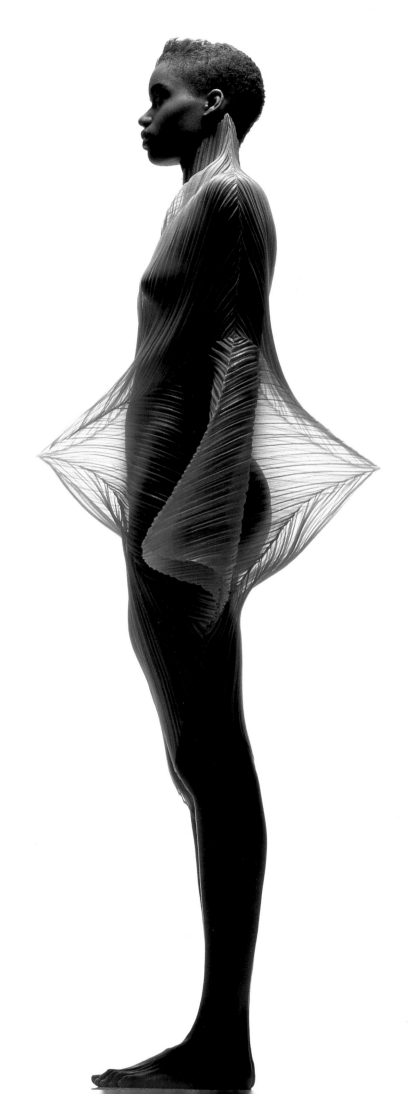

forms with the volume and movements of their bodies while the abstract outlines made geometry on the ground. Just as Miyake's imagination had previously adopted the poetic language of organic forms, these coloured shapes of such deceptive simplicity could touch childhood associations. Miyake's achievement was to render such simplicity with a technology of such complexity. The final decade of a complex century was a moment for the simplicity of Miyake's response. The act of engagement was simply for woman to lift the cloth, find the space for her head and the holes for her arms, then allow her body to fill the space. Miyake refers to cloth that moves like a breeze. The body's breath and movements inflate these simple, flattened shapes into fluid three-dimensions.

The mobility that the pleats offered was repeated with *Twist* in 1992, where the finished garment was twisted and crumpled by hand, granting the human touch to the fabric and developing what the Miyake Design Studio referred to as "the tactile bond between man and clothing". *Twist* became the title for an exhibition at the newly completed museum on Naoshima in the Inland Sea, designed by Tadao Ando. The approach leads to a mooring and up a hillside to the museum, sunken into the ground in a great submerged cylinder. The entrance involves a descent into the earth. The walls are finished with Ando's refined concrete surfaces and a central glass dome illuminates the space. Miyake suspended coloured cords of twisted cloth from the dome to the ground. Transparent mannequins, made from a very light vinyl chloride material, were gathered below, draped in twisted cloth. Garments were laid beside them, flat on the ground in their untwisted state.

Although the demands of the industry require the arrival of a new collection, Miyake is not pressured to invent with every season. A technique such as pleating is modified from year to year, reiterating ongoing design concerns. The pleating, twisting and now, shrinking, continue as further textile possibilities are explored. Beyond the fashion world and the management of a business, Miyake's creativity takes astonishing turns. He created pleated jackets in national colours for the Lithuanian Olympic team at the 1992 Barcelona Olympics. This athletic enthusiasm led to a series of sports outfits in ten national colours under the title *Fiction* in 1993. Dance then became an obvious medium through which to see his designs in motion. His collaborations with the choreographer William Forsythe and the Frankfurt Ballet, initiated in 1991, have continued with his frequent use of dancers from the Frankfurt Ballet performing in the shows of the Miyake collection. In contrast to the still, sculptural quality so elegantly revealed by Irving Penn, the dancers offer him a view of his work in full flight.

hängt die Kleidung an gigantischen Stahlseilen, ein metallener Kontrast zu den Assoziationen der Heian-Periode, die Vreeland beschreibt. Miyakes Schaufensterinstallationen, wie auch die Plakate von Penn, unterstreichen seine Vision mit einer Schlichtheit, die ebenso dramatisch ist wie seine Installationen im Museum. Das Konzept der Gemeinschaftsproduktionen ermöglicht es Miyake, fortwährend öffentlich präsent zu sein. »Das Schlimmste an den Achtzigern war, daß die Designer zu Stars hochgespielt wurden. Design ist keine Erweiterung meines Egos. Design ist Teamarbeit. Ich habe viele Mitarbeiter. Design bedeutet, Verantwortung zu übernehmen.«[8] Für sein Parfum *L'Eau d'Issey*, das im Jahre 1992 auf den Markt kam, kreierte er eine extrem konisch geformte Flasche mit einem kugelförmigen Verschluß. Die Verpackung wurde in Zusammenarbeit mit dem New Yorker Designer Fabien Baron entworfen. Die Detailarbeit bei der Verpackung nahm den gleichen Stellenwert ein wie die Gestaltung eines Schaufensters.

Während der achtziger Jahre führte Miyake nicht nur sein Tokioter Studio, sondern erweiterte seine Rolle zum Kulturunternehmer in Japan. Die Keramiken von Lucy Rie, einer in London lebenden Wiener Emigrantin, hielt er zum Beispiel für »japanischer« als die Teeschalen seiner eigenen Heimat, die stets mit den Assoziationen ihrer eigenen langen Geschichte befrachtet waren. Auf die Initiative Miyakes hin fand 1987 am Sogetsu Kaikan, dem Zentrum traditioneller japanischer Kunst in Tokio, eine Ausstellung der Werke von Lucy Rie statt. Der Architekt Tadao Ando hatte ihre Arbeiten auf Wasser installiert. Im darauffolgenden Jahr brachte Miyake zusammen mit Eiko Ishioka und Shiro Kuramata Marcel L'Herbiers lang verschollenen Stummfilm *L'Inhumaine* von 1923 in der Bunkamura Orchard Hall in Tokio zur Aufführung. Miyake wurde über seine Rolle als Designer hinaus zum aktiven Kulturvermittler, der, Hindernisse überwindend, die Kultur von Keramik bis zum Kino förderte.

Die Ausstellung *A-ŪN* hatte eine völlige Umorientierung in Miyakes Entwicklungsweg zur Folge. Die Besucherzahlen der Ausstellung in Paris waren immens. Der Fotoband von Penn brachte Miyakes spektakuläre Entwürfe zur vollen Geltung. Die Umsetzung der Schau war fantastisch gelungen, Miyake wußte aber, daß zwar »viele Leute zum Schauen kamen, doch nur wenige zum Tragen«. Wieder einmal verlagerte er seinen Schwerpunkt von extravaganter zu tragbarer Kleidung.

1988, im selben Jahr wie die Ausstellung *A-ŪN*, begannen auch seine Experimente mit gefältelten, knitterigen Stoffen. Bereits 1975 hatte er mit gefälteltem Leinenkrepp experimentiert. Bei dem mit Polyurethanschaumstoff überzogenen Jerseyrock, den das Mannequin auf dem Cover von *Artforum* 1982 zum berühmten Rattan-Oberteil getragen hatte, handelte

tout un travail d'équipe et je suis aidé par de nombreux collaborateurs. Le design, c'est une grande responsabilité.»[8] Pour son parfum *L'Eau d'Issey*, lancé en 1992, Miyake a dessiné un flacon inédit, de forme conique, coiffé d'un bouchon sphérique. Le packaging a été réalisé avec la collaboration du designer new-yorkais Fabien Baron. Pour Miyake, l'aspect esthétique du produit est aussi important que la vitrine où il est exposé.

Tout au long des années 80, Miyake continue de créer dans son studio, tout en élargissant son rôle d'ambassadeur culturel à l'intérieur du Japon. Il fait connaître les céramiques de Lucy Rie, une Viennoise réfugiée à Londres dont les œuvres lui paraissent plus «japonaises» que les bols à thé de son propre pays, pourtant chargés d'une longue histoire. En 1987, sur son initiative, une exposition sur l'eau de ces pièces, mise en scène par l'architecte Tadao Ando, est organisée au Sogetsu Kaikan, le centre esthétique traditionnel de Tokyo. L'année suivante, Miyake, Eiko Ishioka et Shiro Kuramata s'associent pour présenter et projeter au Bunkamura Orchard Hall de Tokyo un chef-d'œuvre du cinéma muet tombé depuis longtemps dans l'oubli, *L'Inhumaine* de Marcel L'Herbier (1923). Dépassant son rôle de créateur de mode en défendant des causes insolites et variées, de la céramique au cinéma, Miyake entend ainsi devenir un véritable «pont» culturel, capable de faire tomber toutes les barrières traditionnelles.

Après l'exposition *A-ŪN*, Miyake décide de changer de direction. Le public parisien s'est déplacé en masse pour admirer ses modèles, ses spectaculaires créations ont été glorifiées par les photos de Penn, ses décors sont extraordinaires. Mais Miyake sait bien que, même s'il a de nombreux admirateurs, peu de gens osent porter ses tenues. Une fois encore, il décide de s'écarter du fantastique pour se rapprocher du quotidien et du pratique.

En 1988, l'année même de l'exposition parisienne, Miyake commence à travailler le plissé. En 1975 déjà, il en avait exploré les possibilités avec des crêpes de lin blanc. La jupe en jersey enduite de polyuréthane qui accompagnait le fameux bustier de rotin paru en couverture de *Artforum* était déjà plissée. La technique des plis remonte à la civilisation égyptienne. Et le grand couturier vénitien Mariano Fortuny s'est distingué dès le début du siècle par ses célèbres plissés réalisés dans de fines étoffes de soie. Pour Miyake, les plis sont la conclusion logique de sa recherche du vêtement fonctionnel et de sa passion pour la surface de l'étoffe. Il commence par les expérimenter sur des tissus extensibles et propose des bodies décorés, ressemblant à sa «seconde peau» tatouée des années 70. Mais ces modèles en tissu stretch n'attirent qu'une clientèle limitée. Il décide donc de se servir de coton ou de polyester tissés, puis de tricot jersey pour que l'effet de plis soit comme accompagné, renforcé par

Issey Miyake Pleats Please Exhibition
1990, Tokyo
Photo: © S. Anzai

Page 86/87 · Seite 86/87
Tattoo Body
Autumn/Winter 1989/90
Photo: Oliviero Toscani for *Stern*
Page 90/91/92
Seite 90/91/92
Energieën Exhibition
1990, Amsterdam
Photo: © S. Anzai
Page 93 · Seite 93
Rhythm Pleats
Spring/Summer 1990
Photo: Richard Haughton
Page 94/95 · Seite 94/95
Pleats Please
Photo: Kazumi Kurigami
Page 96/97 · Seite 96/97
Pleats Please
Spring/Summer 1993
Photo: Yasuaki Yoshinaga
Page 98/99 · Seite 98/99
Pleats Please Catalogue
Spring/Summer 1994
Page 100/101 · Seite 100/101
Twists
Spring/Summer 1992
Photo: Kazumi Kurigami

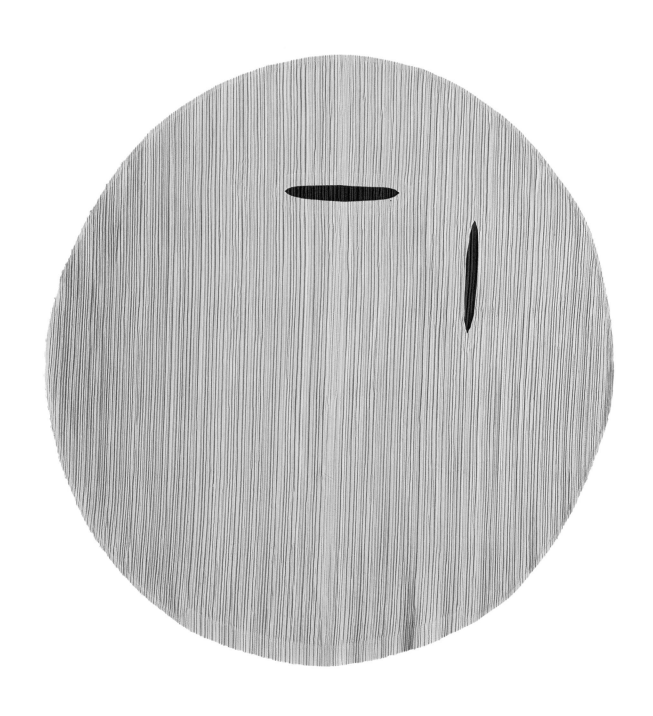

Issey Miyake Twist Exhibition
1992, Benesse House/Naoshima Contemporary
Art Museum; Architect: Tadao Ando
Photo: © S. Anzai

The preoccupation with simplicity of form is shared with the sculptor Isamu Noguchi, who was Miyake's friend. Noguchi suffered from the East/West divide in an earlier generation when his work was considered too Japanese for the Japanese in the immediate postwar years. He later transcended prejudice with universal and monumental work, constantly returning to elemental shapes. One of his last sculptures sits in the courtyard of the Miyake Design Studio.

Miyake creates contradictions. He has destroyed boundaries – those that separate fashion from the world of design, as well as those that lie between East and West. Yet he has declared his desire to maintain boundaries, albeit transparent walls through which we glimpse foreign cultures and colour. Design is the language with which this exchange takes place and the Miyake Design Studio is the creative axis enabling the exchange.

The Miyake Design Studio is the research base, but it also serves as a place for the development of talent. Miyake's career has been built through constant collaboration. From the outset Makiko Minagawa, the textile designer, has played a central role in Miyake's work. Beside her, Tomio Mohri worked on the knitwear and the development of costume design and theatre projects. Kosuke Tsumura works on designs for *Plantation* as well as independently for his own line *K-Zelle*. Akira Onozuka, who was Miyake's Associate Designer from the late Seventies to the late Eighties, now has his own line, *Zucca*. Naoki Takizawa is bringing a new approach to the studio in the Nineties by expanding the use of technology and finding industrial bases for new manufacturing techniques. Kazuhiro Dohman is acting in collaboration between the studio and other companies applying new technologies to tools for contemporary business from bags or stationary to computer software.

However constant Miyake's preoccupation with the traditional and the modern might be, his inventions and re-inventions are born in the shifting climate of the Miyake Design Studio as it adapts to the creative and technical possiblities of the moment. In a recent lecture Miyake explained how new technology in fact became the means through which tradition was preserved, "Traditional hand-craftsmanship all over the world must continue to be appreciated by all people, not just the chosen few. The only way to achieve this is by making tradition modern through technology. If we cannot make traditions suitable for today's lifestyle, in function and in price, then the traditions will eventually die out."[10]

Miyake has grounded his design in simple function, making "clothes for living". Yet he has drawn on imagery of a poetic language with suggestions of light, wind, and the shapes of plants and creatures. He is playfully futuristic with "flying saucers" and robustly

es sich um einen Faltenrock. Historisch gesehen reicht die Technik des Fältelns bis ins alte Ägypten zurück. In der Neuzeit hatte sich der venezianische Künstler Mariano Fortuny um die Jahrhundertwende mit kostbaren gefältelten Seidenroben einen Namen gemacht. Für Miyake waren Falten ebenso das Ergebnis seiner Suche nach funktionaler Kleidung wie seiner Faszination von der Struktur des Materials. Anfangs experimentierte er mit Stretch-Stoffen und brachte Body-Stockings auf den Markt, die wie die Entwürfe seiner »zweiten Haut« mit Tätowierungen bedruckt waren. Doch der Absatzmarkt dafür war begrenzt. Danach entwickelte er Falten in einem Baumwoll- und Polyestergewebe, später in Jersey, bei dem die Falten mit der natürlichen Elastizität der Wirkware einhergingen. Das Ergebnis war der Entwurf seiner Linie *Pleats Please* aus dem Jahre 1988. Er verwendete nach elementaren Formen geschnittene Polyesterstoffe und wandelte jedes Jahr die Farbschattierungen ab. *Pleats Please* war Miyakes schlichteste Kollektion. Leicht tragbar und einfach zu waschen, eignete sie sich ideal als Reisebekleidung für das moderne Zeitalter. *Pleats Please* wird heutzutage in der ganzen Welt vermarktet. Abwandlungen folgten, die die Tragbarkeit mit immer neuen visuellen Effekten verbanden. »Falten bewegen sich und verändern ihre Form mit den Körperbewegungen des Trägers. Wenn sich die Falten bewegen, changieren die Farben und erzeugen eine optische Täuschung ähnlich der eines Kaleidoskops«, erklärte er. »Falten können mich stets aufs neue faszinieren und rufen vielfältige Bilder hervor.«[9] Anders als die übliche Methode, Polyester unter Hitzeeinwirkung zu fälteln und dann erst zuzuschneiden, drehte Miyake den Prozeß um: Er entwarf zuerst den Schnitt, und der fertige Zuschnitt wurde anschließend gefältelt. Die Faltenpresse avancierte zum Fokus für die Experimente mit unterschiedlichen Materialzusammenstellungen: Kompositionen aus Wolle, Leinen und Baumwolle wurden ebenso ausprobiert wie Variationen im Farbton der Stoffe. Der ursprüngliche grafische Effekt bestand in der Kombination aus horizontalen und vertikalen Linien. Indem man aber den Stoff wendete und seitlich in die Faltenpresse schob, ergaben sich Kleider mit einem diagonalen Falteneffekt. Diese Methode bedeutete nicht nur zusätzliche Elastizität für den Träger, sondern auch ein unablässig changierendes Farbenspiel im Licht. Miyakes Sensibilität für die Stoffoberfläche wurde damit verstärkt.

Miyake hatte gehofft, daß gerade Kinder Gefallen an der einfachen Geometrie seiner Ausstellung *Pleats Please,* im Touko Museum of Modern Art 1990 in Tokio, fänden. Die Knitterkleider waren als abstrakte Formen flach ausgebreitet und in den Fußboden eingelassen. Die Besucher zogen ihre Schuhe aus und liefen über die Ovale und Rechtecke aus gelbem, rotem, ockerfarbenem oder schwarzem Stoff. Eine ähnliche Installa-

l'extensibilité du jersey. Sa recherche aboutit au lancement de la ligne *Pleats Please* en 1988, de coupes ultra-simples conçues dans un tissu en polyester; tous les ans, il y ajoute de nouvelles nuances. La ligne *Pleats Please* regroupe les modèles les plus purs de Miyake. Légères, faciles d'entretien, ces tenues sont idéales. Aujourd'hui, *Pleats Please* est commercialisés dans le monde entier. Les modèles, bien sûr, ont légèrement évolué mais ils restent toujours pratiques, agréables et surprenants. «Les plis bougent et se métamorphosent à chaque mouvement du corps. Au fil de leurs mouvements, les couleurs changent, créant une illusion d'optique semblable à celle d'un kaléidoscope», explique le créateur. «Les plis ont le pouvoir de me fasciner et d'évoquer en moi une multitude d'images.»[9] Rejetant les méthodes classiques qui consistent à plisser le polyester par chauffage avant de couper le tissu, Miyake préfère couper d'abord et plisser ensuite. Avec la presse à plisser, Miyake explore diverses alliances de tissus, joue avec la laine, le lin, le coton, et une infinie variété de couleurs et d'épaisseurs. A l'origine, l'effet graphique était essentiellement produit par des lignes horizontales et verticales, mais en orientant différemment le tissu dès son entrée dans la machine, Miyake obtient d'inédites diagonales. Ce type de plissé, tout en procurant un plus grand confort à celle qui le porte, accroche et fait jouer la lumière, exaltant ainsi la surface de l'étoffe. Miyake était certain que les enfants apprécieraient le caractère géométrique de son exposition *Pleats Please* qui se tient en 1990 au Touko, le Musée d'Art Contemporain de Tokyo. Reprenant les mêmes idées que celles de l'exposition *Energieën* au Musée Stedelijk d'Amsterdam, au début de la même année, Miyake y expose ses robes plissées mais à plat, comme incrustées dans le sol de la galerie. Les visiteurs se déchaussent et défilent tout autour d'ovales et rectangles d'étoffes jaunes, pourpres, ocres et noires. Lors de l'inauguration, les mêmes robes apparaissent portées par des invitées qui animent de leur corps et de leurs mouvements les formes abstraites que l'on peut voir au sol. De même que l'imagination de Miyake lui a fait adopter le langage poétique de la forme organique, de même ces taches colorées à l'apparente simplicité peuvent rappeler des dessins d'enfants. Et la force du créateur, c'est précisément d'avoir réussi à donner une impression de simplicité en utilisant pourtant une technique extrêmement sophistiquée.

La dernière décennie de ce siècle complexe convient idéalement aux recherches d'épuration de Miyake. Avec lui, le geste de la femme consiste essentiellement à soulever la toile, à trouver le trou correspondant à la tête et aux bras, puis à laisser son corps donner le volume adéquat à l'ensemble. Miyake parle d'un tissu qui ondoie comme la brise. Le souffle et les mouvements du corps «gonflent» ces formes plates en

Jessye Norman, 1993
Photo: Brigitte Lacombe

Mischa Maisky, 1993
Photo: Julian Broad for
Harper's Queen

Page 106 · Seite 106
Black Lantern
Spring/Summer 1993
Photo: Tyen

traditional with farm-workers' cloth and so, like all artists, he reinvents the present. Through a series of steps, with deceptive ease, he can transform an archaic form, such as the pleat, into a working style for the next century.

Notes:
Unless otherwise stated, all quotes from Issey Miyake are derived from an interview by Mark Holborn, Tokyo, November 1993.

1. The Blackburn Lectures, Central Saint Martin's College of Art and Design, London, October 25, 1993.
2. A Poem of Cloth and Stone, Tokyo, 1963.
3. Aromu Mushiake, Sports Nippon, July 13, 1977.
4. Japan Today, lecture, San Francisco, September 1983. See also Jun I. Kanai, Fuku (clothing) which brings Fuku (happiness), Ten Sen Men, Hiroshima, 1990.
5. Artforum, editorial by Ingrid Sischy and Germano Celant, New York, February 1992.
6. Lecture, Los Angeles County Museum, 1987. See also Jun I. Kanai, Fuku (clothing) which brings Fuku (happiness), Ten Sen Men, Hiroshima, 1990.
7. Issey Miyake East Meets West, Tokyo, 1978.
8. Marie Claire, June 1992.
9. Ten Sen Men, Hiroshima, 1990.
10. Lecture, New York Public Library, 1994.

tion hatte er im selben Jahr bereits im Stedelijk Museum in Amsterdam als Beitrag zur Ausstellung *Energieën* realisiert. Bei der Vernissage in Tokio erschienen Gäste in den ausgestellten Knitterkleidern und füllten die flachen, zweidimensionalen Formen mit Volumen und den Bewegungen ihrer Körper, während die abstrakten Umrisse am Boden ein geometrisches Muster ergaben. Ähnlich wie sich Miyakes Imagination zuvor der poetischen Sprache organischer Formen bedient hatte, konnten diese bunten Gebilde trügerischer Einfachheit Assoziationen an die Kindheit hervorrufen. Miyakes Verdienst war es, jene Schlichtheit der Form mit einer so aufwendigen Technik zu erzielen. Das letzte Jahrzehnt eines komplexen Jahrhunderts war der geeignete Moment für Miyakes Reduktionen. Alles was von der Trägerin verlangt wurde, war, das Stück Stoff hochzuheben, den Ausschnitt für den Kopf und die Löcher für die Arme zu finden, um dann mit ihrem Körper den Platz auszufüllen. Miyake spricht von Stoff, der sich bewegt wie ein Windhauch. Atmung und Bewegung des Körpers hauchen diesen einfachen, flachen Formen dreidimensionale Lebendigkeit ein.

Die Vielfältigkeit der Knitterstoffe wurde mit der Linie *Twist* im Jahre 1992 erneut unter Beweis gestellt. Der fertige Stoff wurde von Hand gewrungen und geknittert, was dem Material eine menschliche Note verlieh. Hieraus entstand das, was das Miyake Design Studio als »taktiles Band zwischen Mensch und Kleidung« bezeichnete. *Twist* war auch der Titel einer Ausstellung im neu errichteten Museum auf Naoshima im japanischen Biwa-See, das Tadao Ando entworfen hatte. Der Weg zum Museum führt von einem Ankerplatz einen Hügel hinauf, das Museum selbst steht wie ein riesiger überschwemmter Zylinder im Boden versenkt. Beim Eingang steigt man in die Erde hinab. Den Wänden hat Ando mit verfeinerten Betonoberflächen den letzten Schliff gegeben. Durch eine Glaskuppel in der Mitte wird der Raum erhellt. Miyake ließ farbige Seile aus Knitterstoff von der Kuppel auf den Boden hinabhängen. Unten drängten sich durchsichtige Schaufensterpuppen aus einem sehr leichten Vinylchlorid, eingehüllt in knittrigen Stoff. Neben ihnen waren die Kleidungsstücke in ihrem ungeknitterten Zustand flach auf dem Boden ausgebreitet.

Obwohl die Modebranche jede Saison eine neue Kollektion erwartet, ist Miyake nicht gezwungen, sich diesem Rhythmus zu unterwerfen. Er wandelt ein bereits bestehendes Konzept, wie zum Beispiel das der Knitterstoffe, von Jahr zu Jahr ab und entwickelt es so weiter. Nach wie vor wird mit der Vorbehandlung der Textilien experimentiert: Die Stoffe werden geknittert, gewrungen und nun auch durch Vorwaschen bei hohen Temperaturen geschrumpft.

Miyakes Kreativität findet über das Management seines Modeimperiums hinaus erstaunliche Betätigungsfelder außerhalb der Welt der Mode. Anläßlich

leur donnant une nouvelle fluidité et une troisième dimension.

Avec la ligne *Twist* (1992), le Miyake Design Studio continue à exploiter la mobilité des plissés en tordant et en froissant le vêtement fini à la main dans le but de donner à l'étoffe une touche plus humaine, d'établir un «lien tactile entre l'être et le vêtement». Le mot *Twist* devient également le titre d'une exposition au nouveau Musée de Naoshima (dessiné par Tadao Ando) au cœur de la Mer Intérieure. Après avoir débarqué sur l'île, le visiteur doit grimper une colline pour découvrir le bâtiment, immense cylindre souterrain auquel on accède en redescendant vers les entrailles de la terre. Les murs sont recouverts de bas-reliefs en béton créés par Ando et l'intérieur est éclairé par un dôme de verre central. De cette coupole, Miyake laisse pendre jusqu'au sol de longs cordages colorés, faits d'étoffes tordues. Dessous: un groupe de mannequins ultra-légers en vinyle transparent drapés dans ce même tissu. Les vêtements non encore tordus sont disposés à côté, à même le sol.

Même si le marché exige sans cesse de nouvelles collections, Miyake refuse de se soumettre aux pressions en inventant une nouvelle ligne chaque saison. Ses techniques, tel le plissé, évoluent d'année en année mais il reprend des styles déjà bien établis. Il préfère continuer à exploiter les possibilités textiles du plissé, du tordage, du «rétréci». Ignorant les exigences de la mode et des affaires, la créativité de Miyake prend d'étonnantes directions. Ainsi, à l'occasion des Jeux Olympiques de Barcelone en 1992, il crée pour l'équipe de Lituanie des vestes plissées aux couleurs nationales. Cet enthousiasme pour l'athlétisme l'amène à créer en 1993 toute une série de tenues sportives pour une dizaine de nations. C'est la ligne *Fiction*.

La danse devient bientôt l'un de ses «véhicules» préférés, car elle lui permet de montrer ses modèles en mouvement. En 1991, il commence à collaborer avec le chorégraphe William Forsythe et le ballet de Francfort. Depuis, les artistes de cette troupe ont souvent porté ses vêtements. Les danseurs offrent un aspect de son œuvre en plein essor, en contraste frappant avec l'élégance sculpturale et hiératique photographiée par Irving Penn.

Cette obsession de la simplicité, Miyake la partage avec son ami sculpteur Isamu Noguchi. Ce dernier a souffert de la césure entre Est et Ouest dans les années d'après-guerre. Même les Japonais jugeaient son œuvre trop japonaise. Plus tard, avec ses sculptures universelles et monumentales revenant constamment aux formes élémentaires, il arrive à vaincre ces préjugés. L'une de ses œuvres les plus récentes se trouve dans le patio du Miyake Design Studio. Issey Miyake engendre la contradiction. Il a fait tomber des barrières, celles qui séparaient le monde de la mode du monde des arts, celles qui séparaient l'Est de

"The Loss of Small Detail"
William Forsythe & Frankfurt Ballet
1993, Tokyo
Photo: Kyoji Akiba

der Olympischen Spiele in Barcelona 1992 entwarf er für die Delegation aus Litauen Blazer aus Knitterstoff in den Nationalfarben. 1993 schuf er die Linie *Fiction,* eine Serie von Trikots in zehn verschiedenen Nationalfarben. Es lag nahe, daß sich Miyake nach dem Bereich des Sports nun dem Tanz zuwenden würde, um dort seine Entwürfe in Bewegung zu sehen. Seit 1991 arbeitet Miyake mit dem Choreographen William Forsythe und dem Frankfurter Ballett zusammen. Des öfteren treten Tänzer der Frankfurter Truppe auch als Mannequins in seinen Modenschauen auf. Im Gegensatz zu der unbewegten Skulpturenhaftigkeit, die Irving Penn in den Fotos der Miyake-Entwürfe so elegant zum Ausdruck brachte, verleihen die Tänzer seinen Kleidern eine atemberaubende Beweglichkeit.

Das Interesse an der Reduktion der Form teilt Miyake mit dem Bildhauer Isamu Noguchi, mit dem er befreundet war. Noguchi hatte unter dem Ost-West-Konflikt bereits eine Generation früher zu leiden. In den Jahren unmittelbar nach dem Krieg galt sein Werk in Japan als zu japanisch. Später konnte er sich durch die universale und monumentale Gestaltung seiner Arbeiten, die sich auf ganz elementare Formen stützte, von diesem Vorurteil befreien. Eine seiner letzten Skulpturen steht im Innenhof des Miyake Design Studios.

Miyake schafft Widersprüche. Er hat Grenzen überwunden: nicht nur die, welche Modewelt und Design auseinanderhalten, sondern auch die, die Osten und Westen trennen. Trotzdem hat er sich zum erklärten Befürworter von Grenzen gemacht, aber nur im Sinne durchsichtiger Mauern, durch die wir einen Blick auf fremde Kulturen und Farben werfen können. Design fungiert als Sprache, mit deren Hilfe dieser Austausch gelingt, und das Miyake Design Studio bildet die kreative Basis dieses Austausches. Das Miyake Design Studio ist ein Platz für Experimente, aber auch ein Ort, an dem Talente sich entfalten können. Miyakes Werdegang gründet auf kontinuierlicher Zusammenarbeit. Von Anfang an hatte die Textildesignerin Makiko Minagawa bei Miyakes Arbeiten eine Schlüsselrolle inne. Neben ihr arbeitete Tomio Mohri bei den Strickkollektionen mit, beim Design von Kostümen und der Konzeption von Theaterprojekten. Kosuke Tsumura lieferte Entwürfe für *Plantation,* aber auch für seine eigene Kollektion *K-Zelle.* Akira Onozuka, der heute seine eigene Kollektion *Zucca* hat, war Miyakes kreativer Partner von den späten Siebzigern bis zum Ende der achtziger Jahre. Für die neunziger Jahre hat Naoki Takizawa eine neue Richtung im Studio eingeschlagen: die stärkere Anwendung moderner Technologien und die Suche nach Produktionsstätten für neue Herstellungsmethoden. Kazuhiro Dohman wendet in Zusammenarbeit von Studio und anderen Firmen neue Technologien in der Herstellung von Handtaschen, Schreibwaren bis hin zu Computer-Software an. Miyake hat sich fortwährend mit Tradition und

l'Ouest. Cependant, s'il proclame son désir de maintenir certaines démarcations, il désire que celles-ci ne soient plus que des cloisons transparentes à travers lesquelles chacun pourrait contempler d'autres cultures, d'autres nuances. Le design est le langage qui rend possible cet échange; le Miyake Design Studio est le meilleur de ses outils.

Le Miyake Design Studio est un centre de recherche mais c'est également le berceau où bien des talents vont grandir et se développer. La carrière de Miyake s'établit sur la base d'une constante collaboration avec d'autres créateurs. Ainsi, dès le début, la dessinatrice textile Makiko Minagawa tient une place importante dans l'équipe de Miyake. A ses côtés, il y avait également Tomio Mohri, qui travaillait dans le secteur du tricot et créait des costumes de théâtre. Kosuke Tsumura collabora à la collection *Plantation* tout en dessinant aussi sa propre griffe, *K-Zelle.* Akira Onozuka, qui possède maintenant sa marque, *Zucca,* fut styliste assistant de Miyake à la fin des années 70 et jusqu'à la fin des années 80. Aujourd'hui, c'est Naoki Takizawa qui met son empreinte sur le studio en lui donnant une nouvelle orientation, plus en harmonie avec notre décennie: s'appuyant davantage sur la technologie, il trouve des bases industrielles adaptées aux nouvelles méthodes de fabrication. Kazuhiro Dohman s'occupe des projets de collaboration du studio avec diverses entreprises qui appliquent des procédés de fabrication avancés aux fournitures commerciales – de la papeterie aux sacs, en passant par les logiciels. Cependant, même si la volonté d'associer tradition et modernité reste constante chez Miyake, ses inventions et réinventions naissent dans le climat turbulent du Miyake Design Studio, qui profite aussi de toutes les possibilités créatives et techniques du moment. Dans une récente conférence, Miyake a expliqué comment les nouvelles technologies sont en fait devenues le moyen de préserver la tradition: «L'artisanat traditionnel, partout dans le monde, doit être mis à la portée de tous et ne doit pas être réservé à quelques privilégiés. Seule la technologie nous permettra de ‹moderniser› les trésors que les siècles nous ont légués. Si nous ne sommes pas capables de l'adapter aux exigences de la vie moderne, de la rendre plus fonctionnelle et moins onéreuse, la tradition disparaîtra à tout jamais.»

Miyake base son style sur le fonctionnel et préfère concevoir des «vêtements à vivre». Pourtant, il s'inspire d'une imagerie et d'un langage poétique qui évoquent la lumière, le vent, les plantes, les animaux. Si avec ses soucoupes volantes il joue la carte du futurisme, avec ses étoffes campagnardes, en revanche, il montre son attachement à la tradition. Ainsi, comme tous les artistes, il réinvente le présent. Par une douce progression, avec une apparente aisance, il sait faire d'un procédé archaïque comme le plissé un style parfaitement adapté à la vie active de demain.

Moderne beschäftigt, seine Erfindungen und Wiederentdeckungen aber entstehen in der Atmosphäre des Studios, die sich mit den künstlerischen und technischen Möglichkeiten der Zeit wandelt. Kürzlich erklärte Miyake in einem Vortrag, wie gerade neue Technologien zum Mittel werden, die Tradition zu erhalten. »Es ist notwendig, daß auch in Zukunft alle, und nicht nur eine kleine Anzahl Auserwählter, das traditionelle Handwerk überall auf der ganzen Welt zu schätzen wissen. Das kann man nur erreichen, indem man die Tradition mit Hilfe neuer Technik wieder modern macht. Wenn es uns nicht gelingt, die Tradition dem heutigen Lebensstil anzupassen, was Funktion und Preis betrifft, dann kann es sein, daß sie ausstirbt.«[10]

Miyake hat seinem Design eine einfache Funktion zugeschrieben: Er entwirft »Kleidung für das Leben«. Seine Bildersprache dagegen ist poetisch angehaucht, erweckt Assoziationen von Licht, Wind, Pflanzen und Tieren. Er kann gleichermaßen futuristisch sein — mit seinen »fliegenden Untertassen« — wie auch bodenständig und traditionell — mit seinen bäuerlichen Stoffen. Wie alle Künstler zeichnet er damit ein neues Bild der Gegenwart. Mit trügerischer Leichtigkeit gelingt es ihm, eine archaische Form wie die des Faltenwurfs umzusetzen in die Alltagskleidung für das kommende Jahrhundert.

Anmerkungen:
Soweit nicht anders vermerkt, sind alle Zitate von Issey Miyake entnommen aus einem Interview mit Mark Holborn, Tokio, November 1993.
1. The Blackburn Lectures, Central Saint Martin's College of Art and Design, London, 25. Oktober 1993.
2. A Poem of Cloth and Stone, Tokio 1963.
3. Aromu Mushiake, Sports Nippon, 13. Juli 1977.
4. Japan Today, lecture, San Francisco, September 1993. Vgl. auch Jun I. Kanai, Fuku (clothing), which brings Fuku (happiness), Ten Sen Men, Hiroshima 1990.
5. Artforum, Editorial by Ingrid Sischy and Germano Celant, New York, Februar 1992.
6. Lecture, Los Angeles County Museum, 1978. Vgl. auch Jun I. Kanai, Fuku (clothing), which brings Fuku (happiness), Ten Sen Men, Hiroshima 1990.
7. Issey Miyake East Meets West, Tokio 1978.
8. Marie Claire, Juni 1992.
9. Ten Sen Men, Hiroshima 1990.
10. Vortrag in der New Yorker Public Library, 1994.

Notes finales:
Sauf indications contraires, toutes les citations d'Issey Miyake proviennent d'une interview réalisée par Mark Holborn à Tokyo en novembre 1993.
1. The Blackburn Lectures, Central Saint Martin's College of Art and Design, Londres, 25 octobre 1993.
2. A Poem of Cloth and Stone, Tokyo, 1963
3. Aromu Mushiake, Sports Nippon, 13 juillet 1977.
4. Japan today, conférence, San Francisco, septembre 1983. Voir également Jun I. Kanai, Fuku (l'habillement) qui apporte Fuku (le bonheur), ten Sen Men, Hiroshima, 1990.
5. Artforum, Editorial d'Ingrid Sischy et Germano Celant, New York, février 1992.
6. Conférence, Los Angeles County Museum, 1987. Voir également Jun I. Kanai Fuku (l'habillement) qui apporte Fuku (le bonheur), Ten Sen Men, Hiroshima, 1990.
7. Issey Miyake East Meets West, Tokyo, 1978.
8. Marie-Claire, juin 1992.
9. Ten Sen Men, Hiroshima 1990.
10. Conférence, Bibliothèque publique de New York, 1994.

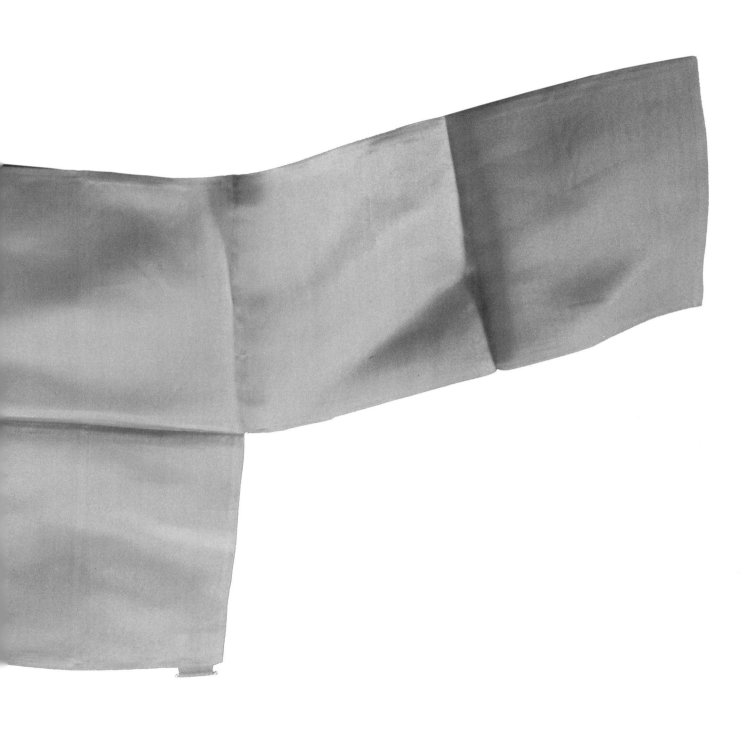

Paris Collection
Autumn/Winter 1995/96
Jacqueline Jaco-Mica,
Elisabeth Kaza, Claire Lauret-
Bougaran, Andreé Saldo,
Yvonne Wingerter Heitz
Photo: Philippe Brazil

4 ▶ 4A 5 ▶ 5Á 6
10   GOLD 400-4   11   KODAK 400-4   12

10 ▶ 10A 11 ▶ 11A 12
16   GOLD 400-4   17   KODAK 400-4   18

16 ▶ 16A 17 ▶ 17A 18
22   GOLD 400-4   23   KODAK 400-4   24

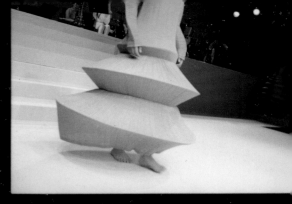

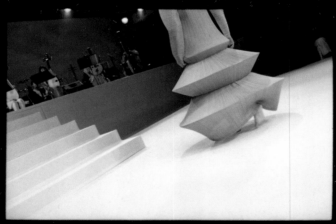

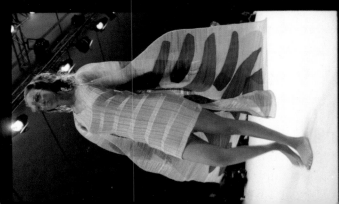

CHRONOLOGY

Elle (France) Cover, 1973
Sashiko & Knit

ISSEY MIYAKE

1938
Born April 22, Hiroshima, Japan

1963
First Collection, *A Poem of Cloth and Stone*, Tokyo

1964
Graduated in graphic design, Tama Art University, Tokyo

1965–1969
Studied and worked in Paris and New York

1970
Hostess uniforms for Expo '70 in Osaka, on behalf of Shiseido

The Toray Knit Exhibit, Tokyo, sponsored by The Toray Corporation

Miyake Design Studio (MDS), Tokyo established

1971
Issey Miyake International Inc. (IMI), established

Press offices established, New York and Paris

First collection, Spring/Summer 1971, New York

Autumn/Winter 1971/72 collection, at opening of Japan House Gallery, New York

Autumn/Winter 1971/72 collection, car parking building of Seibu department store, Shibuya, Tokyo

1972
What is Bodywear? show, Tokyo

1938
Geboren am 22. April in Hiroshima, Japan

1963
Erste Modenschau, *A Poem of Cloth and Stone,* Tokio

1964
Graphikdiplom an der Tama Art University, Tokio

1965–1969
Studium und Arbeit in Paris und New York

1970
Hostessen-Kleidung für Expo '70, Osaka, im Auftrag von Shiseido

The Toray Knit Exhibit von Toray Corporation, Tokio

Gründung des Miyake Design Studios (MDS) in Tokio

1971
Gründung von Issey Miyake International Inc. (IMI)

Gründung der Pressebüros in New York und Paris

Frühjahr/Sommer-Kollektion 1971 in New York

Herbst/Winter-Kollektion 1971/72 anläßlich der Eröffnung der Japan House Gallery in New York

Modenschau im Parkhaus des Seibu Kaufhauses in Shibuya, Tokio

1972
What ist Bodywear? Modenschau in Tokio

1938
Né le 22 avril, à Hiroshima au Japon

1963
Première collection, *A Poem of Cloth and Stone* à Tokyo

1964
Diplômé en dessin graphique, Tama Art University de Tokyo

1965–1969
Etudie et travaille à Paris et New York

1970
Dessine l'uniforme Shiseido, pour l'Expo '70 à Osaka

The Toray Knit Exhibit pour Toray, Tokyo

Création du Miyake Design Studio, Tokyo

1971
Fonde la société Issey Miyake International Inc. (IMI)

Ouvre des bureaux à New York et à Paris

Première collection, Printemps/Eté 1971, New York

Collection Automne/Hiver 1971/72, à l'ouverture de la Japan House Gallery, New York

Collection Automne/Hiver 1971/72, dans le parking du grand magasin Seibu à Shibuya, Tokyo

1972
Show *What is Bodywear?*, Tokyo

Issey Miyake Boutique
From-1st Building, Minami-aoyama, Tokyo,
designed by Shiro Kuramata, 1976
Photo: Fujitsuka Mitsumasa

1973
Elle magazine cover, Paris, features *Sashiko* quilt by Miyake

Colletion moved from New York to Paris, where it continues to be shown twice a year

1974
Issey with Kansai show, Olympic Youth Centre, Tokyo

First boutique opened, Aoyama, Tokyo

Fusae Ichikawa, first Japanese woman member of parliament, photographed in Miyake *Sashiko* for *Asahi Graph*, Tokyo

Received Japan Fashion Editor's Club Award

1975
The Issey Miyake Show, Seibu Theater, Shibuya Parco, Tokyo

Brought Diana Vreeland's exhibition, *Inventive Chlothes 1909–1939* from The Metropolitan Museum of Art, New York, to National Museum of Modern Art, Kyoto

First boutique in Paris established at Place du Marché-Saint-Honoré

1976
Iseey Miyake and Twelve Black Girls show, Tokyo and Osaka

Collection shown at The Fashion Institute of Technology, New York

1973
Elle bringt Miyakes *Sashiko*-Steppstoff auf der Titelseite

Verlegung der Kollektionsschauen von New York nach Paris

1974
Issey with Kansai Schau im Olympic Youth Centre, Tokio

Eröffnung der ersten Issey Miyake Boutique in Aoyama, Tokio

Fusae Ichikawa, erste weibliche Parlamentsabgeordnete Japans, wird in Miyakes *Sashiko*-Kleidung für *Asahi Graph,* Tokio, fotografiert

Erhält den Japan Fashion Editor's Club Award

1975
The Issey Miyake Show im Seibu Theater, Shibuya Parco, Tokio

Miyake bringt Diana Vreelands Ausstellung *Inventive Clothes 1909–1939* des Metropolitan Museum, New York, nach Kioto ins National Museum of Modern Art

Eröffnung der ersten Issey Miyake Boutique in Paris am Place du Marché-Saint-Honoré

1976
Issey Miyake and Twelve Black Girls, Schau in Tokio und Osaka

Kollektionsvorführung im Fashion Institute of Technology, New York

Eröffnung des Haupthauses, ausgestattet von Shiro Kuramata, in Minami-aoyama, Tokio

1973
Le magazine *Elle*, consacre sa couverture au tissu molletonné de Miyake, le *Sashiko*

La collection se déplace de New York à Paris où elle est reprise deux fois par an

1974
Show *Issey with Kansai*, Olympic Youth Center, Tokyo

Ouverture de la première boutique, Aoyama, Tokyo

Fusae Ichikawa, la première femme japonaise admise à siéger au parlement, est photographiée vêtue d'un costume *Sashiko* de Miyake, pour *Asahi Graph*, Tokyo

Reçoit le Prix de l'Edition de Mode au Japon

1975
The Issey Miyake Show, au Théâtre de Seibu, Shibuya Parco, Tokyo

Fait venir l'exposition de Diana Vreeland, *Inventive Clothes 1909–1939* du Metropolitan Museum de New York au National Museum of Modern Art de Kyoto

Ouvre sa première boutique Place du Marché-Saint-Honoré à Paris

1976
Show *Issey Miyake and Twelve Black Girls*, à Tokyo et à Osaka

Collection présentée au Fashion Institute of Technology, New York

Invitation card
Autumn/Winter 1977/78 collection, Paris
designed by Tadanori Yokoo

MA: Espace-Temps du Japon
Musée des Arts Décoratifs, Paris, 1978
Photo: Shuji Yamada

Main boutique opened in Minami-aoyama, Tokyo, designed by Shiro Kuramata

Established *Issey Miyake Men* line

1977
Received 1976 Mainichi Design Prize, which is given the first time to a fashion designer

A Piece of Cloth show, Seibu Museum of Art, Tokyo

Fly with Issey Miyake show, Meiji Jingu Indoor Field, Tokyo and Kyoto Prefectural Gymnasium

1978
Issey Miyake East Meets West published

Participated in *MA: Espace-Temps du Japon* exhibition, Musée des Arts Décoratifs, Paris, and Cooper-Hewitt Museum, New York

1979
East Meets West show at Aspen International Design Conference

Les Tissus imprimés d'Issey Miyake exhibition, Musée de l'Impression sur Étoffes de Mulhouse, France

1980
Participated in the *Japan Style* exhibition, Victoria and Albert Museum, London

Collaborated with Tomio Mohri on design for costumes for *Casta Diva*, a ballet by Maurice Béjart at Centre Georges Pompidou, Paris

Participated in organisation *Evolution of Fashion: 1835–1895* exhibition at National Museum of Modern Art, Kyoto

Einführung der Kollektion *Issey Miyake Men*

1977
Erhält den 1976 Mainichi Design Prize, der zum ersten Mal an einen Modedesigner vergeben wird

A Piece of Cloth, Präsentation im Seibu Museum of Art, Tokio

Fly with Issey Miyake, Schau im Meiji Jingu Sportstadion, Tokio und im öffentlichen Gymnasium, Kioto

1978
Publikation *Issey Miyake East Meets West*

Teilnahme an der Ausstellung *MA: Espace-Temps du Japon* im Musée des Arts Décoratifs, Paris, und im Cooper-Hewitt Museum, New York

1979
East Meets West, Schau anläßlich der Aspen International Design Conference, USA

Les Tissus imprimé d'Issey Miyake (Druckstoffe von Issey Miyake), Ausstellung im Musée de l'Impression sur Étoffes de Mulhouse, Frankreich

1980
Teilnahme an der Ausstellung *Japan Style* im Victoria and Albert Museum, London

Kostümentwürfe zusammen mit Tomio Mohri für *Casta Diva,* Ballett von Maurice Béjart im Centre Georges Pompidou, Paris

Teilnahme an der Organisation der Ausstellung *Evolution of Fashion: 1835–1895,* im National Museum of Modern Art, Kioto

Ouvre sa boutique mère à Minami-aoyama, Tokyo, décorée par Shiro Kuramata

Crée la ligne *Issey Miyake Men*

1977
Reçoit le Prix du Design Mainichi en 1976

Show *A Piece of Cloth*, Museum of Art de Seibu, Tokyo

Fly with Issey Miyake, Stade couvert de Meiji Jingu, Tokyo, et Gymnase Municipal de Kyoto

1978
Publication du livre *Issey Miyake East Meets West*

Participe à l'exposition *MA: Espace-Temps du Japon*, Musée des Arts Décoratifs, Paris, et Cooper-Hewitt-Museum, New York

1979
Show *East Meets West* à la Conférence Internationale sur le Design à Aspen

Exposition *Les Tissus imprimés d'Issey Miyake*, Musée de l'Impression sur Étoffes de Mulhouse, France

1980
Participe à l'exposition *Japan Style*, au Victoria and Albert Museum de Londres

Collabore avec Tomio Mohri pour créer les costumes de *Casta Diva*, ballet de Maurice Béjart, au Centre Georges Pompidou, Paris

Participe à l'organisation de l'exposition *Evolution de la mode: 1835–1895* au National Museum of Modern Art

Live Installation Part 1
Spring/Summer 1984
Photo: Tutomu Wakatsuki

1981

Issey Miyake: It's so Neat show, with young models auditioned from the public, Tokyo and Osaka

Body and Soul in Cloth show, at invitation of Holland Art Directors' Club, Amsterdam

Plantation line established

1982

Artforum magazine cover and editiorial

Participated in *Intimate Architecture: Contemporary Clothing Design* exhibition, Massachusetts Institute of Technology, Cambridge, MA

Issey and Kenzo show, Tokyo and Osaka

Spring/Summer 1983 collection shown on U.S.S. Intrepid, New York, with *Plantation* line worn by amateur chorus

Video presentation of Spring/Summer 1983 collection, Tokyo

1983

Issey Miyake Spectacle Bodyworks exhibition, La Forêt Iikura Museum, Tokyo; Otis/Parsons Gallery, Los Angeles and San Francisco Museum of Modern Art

Issey Miyake Bodyworks book published

Spring/Summer 1984 collection presented of *Live Installation Part 1*, La Forêt Iikura Museum, Tokyo

1984

Received Neiman-Marcus Award, Dallas, International Award from Fashion Designers Council of America, New York, and Mainichi Fashion Grand Prix, Tokyo

1981

Issey Miyake: *It's so Neat,* Schau mit jungen Laien-Mannequins in Tokio und Osaka

Body and Soul in Cloth Modenschau auf Einladung des Holland Art Directors' Club.

Einführung der Kollektion-Linie *Plantation*

1982

Miyakes Kleiderkunst als Titelgeschichte des Magazins *Artforum*

Teilnahme an der Ausstellung *Intimate Architecture: Contemporary Clothing Design,* Massachusetts Institute of Technology, Cambridge, MA

Issey and Kenzo, Schau in Tokio und Osaka

Schau der Frühjahr/Sommer-Kollektion 1983 und der *Plantation*-Linie, getragen von einem Laienchor, auf dem Flugzeugträger U.S.S. Intrepid im Hudson River, New York

Videopräsentation der Frühjahr/Sommer-Kollektion 1983

1983

Ausstellung *Issey Miyake Spectacle Bodyworks* im La Forêt Iikura Museum, Tokio; Otis/Parsons Gallery, Los Angeles und San Francisco Museum of Modern Art

Publikation von *Issey Miyake Bodyworks*

Frühjahr/Sommer-Kollektion 1984 als *Live Installation Part 1,* La Forêt Iikura Museum, Tokio

1984

Erhält Neiman-Marcus Award, Dallas, International Award des Fashion Designers Council of America, New York, sowie den Mainichi Fashion Grand Prix, Tokio

1981

Issey Miyake: *It's so Neat,* avec de jeunes mannequins pris dans le public, Tokyo et Osaka

Show *Body and Soul in Cloth* à l'invitation du Holland, Art Directors' Club, Amsterdam

Création de la ligne *Plantation*

1982

En couverture et en éditorial du magazine *Artforum*

Participe à l'exposition *Intimate Architecture: Contemporary Clothing Design,* Massachussetts Institute of Technology, Cambridge, MA

Show *Issey and Kenzo,* Tokyo et Osaka

Collection Printemps/Eté 1983 présentée sur le navire de guerre U.S.S. Intrepid, New York avec la ligne *Plantation* portée par un chœur d'amateurs

Présentation vidéo de la collection Printemps/Eté 1983, Tokyo

1983

Exposition *Issey Miyake Spectacle Bodyworks,* La Forêt Iikura Museum, Tokyo; Otis/Parsons Gallery, Museum of Modern Art de Los Angeles et de San Francisco

Publication du livre *Issey Miyake Bodyworks*

Collection Printemps/Eté 1984 présentée en *Live Installation Part 1,* La Forêt Iikura Museum, Tokyo

Page 142 · Seite 142
Issey Miyake Permanente, 1985
worn by Elizabeth Frink
Photo: Snowdon

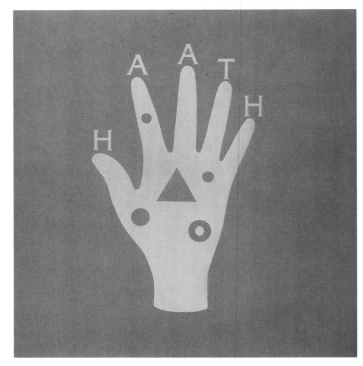

Catalogue cover, *Haath*
art direction by Ikko Tanaka, 1986

Issey Miyake and his Design Workshop, a documentary film broadcast on French state television

Live Installation Part 2 at Laforet Museum, Akasaka, Tokyo

Established *ASHA by MDS*, a collaboration with Asha Sarabhai to extend Indian traditional craft into contemporary design

1985
Issey Miyake Bodyworks: Fashion Without Taboos Exhibition/Boilerhouse Project, Victoria and Albert Museum, London

Appointed first Director of the Concil of Fashion Designers, Tokyo

Les Textiles de l'Inde et les Modèles Créés par Issey Miyake at Musée des Arts Décoratifs, Paris

Received Oscar de la mode Award, Paris.

Published the book *Issey Miyake & Miyake Design Studio 1970–1985*

Time magazine, U.S. edition featured Issey Miyake, October 21

Established *Issey Miyake Permanente* line, featuring classic Miyake design

Spring/Summer 1986 Men's collection *Just a Moment* with Patrick Dupond and Momix dancers at the Centre Georges Pompidou, Paris

1986
Featured as cover story for *Time* magazine, International edition, January 27

Issey Miyake and his Design Workshop, Dokumentarfilm des staatlichen französischen Fernsehens

Live Installation Part 2 im Laforet Museum, Akasaka, Tokio

Gründung von *ASHA by MDS,* eine Zusammenarbeit mit Asha Sarabhai, um das traditionelle indische Kunsthandwerk in zeitgenössisches Design zu integrieren

1985
Issey Miyake Bodyworks: Fashion Without Taboos Exhibition/Boilerhouse Project, Ausstellung im Victoria and Albert Museum, London

Ernennung zum ersten Direktor des Council of Fashion Designers, Tokio

Les Textiles de l'Inde et les Modèles Créés par Issey Miyake, Ausstellung des Musée des Arts Décoratifs, Paris

Erhält den Preis Oscar de la mode, Paris

Publikation *Issey Miyake & Miyake Design Studio 1970–1985*

Issey Miyake als Titelgeschichte der U.S. Ausgabe des *Time* Magazin vom 21. Oktober

Einführung der *Issey Miyake Permanente* Kollektion als klasssische Linie

Just a Moment, Frühjahr/Sommer-Herrenkollektion 1986 vorgeführt mit den Tänzern Patrick Dupond und Momix im Centre Georges Pompidou, Paris

1984
Reçoit le Prix Neiman-Marcus, Dallas, le Prix International décerné par le Comité des Dessinateurs de mode d'Amérique, New York, et le Grand Prix de la mode, Mainichi, Tokyo

Issey Miyake and his Design Workshop, documentaire diffusé à la télévision française

Live Installation Part 2 au Musée Laforet, Akasaka, Tokyo

Lance l'initiative *ASHA by MDS*, en collaboration avec Asha Sarabhai dans le but d'étendre l'art traditionnel indien au dessin contemporain

1985
Issey Miyake Bodyworks: Fashion Without Taboos Exhibition/Boilerhouse Project, Victoria and Albert Museum, Londres

Nommé premier Directeur du Conseil des Dessinateurs de mode, Tokyo

Exposition *Les Textiles de l'Inde et les Modèles Créés par Issey Miyake* au Musée des Arts Décoratifs de Paris

Reçoit l'Oscar de la mode, Paris

Publie le livre *Issey Miyake & Miyake Design Studio, 1970–1985*

Article sur Issey Miyake dans le magazine *Time*, édition U.S., du 21 octobre

Création de la ligne *Issey Miyake Permanente*, conçue dans le Miyake classique

L'Eau d'Issey, 1992
photograph © 1992 Irving Penn

Began collaboration with the photographer, Irving Penn

Organized the exhibition *HAATH, Handwoven Textiles in India and Issey Miyake,* Yurakucho Art Forum, in association with Seibu Museum of Art, Tokyo

1987
Participated in the exhibition *Fashion and Surrealism* at the Fashion Institute of Technology, New York

1988
Issey Miyake A-ŪN exhibition Musée des Arts Décoratifs, Paris

Published the book *Issey Miyake Photographs by Irving Penn*

Received the International Design Grand Award from the Japanese Cultural Design Council and the honorary title of Designer for Industry from the Royal Society of Art, London

Began work on pleats

1989
Issey Miyake Meets Lucie Rie exhibition, Sogetsu Gallery, Tokyo and the Museum of Oriental Ceramics, Osaka

Received the Mainichi Fashion Grand Prix

Received the Officier de l'Ordre des Arts et des Lettres from Jack Lang, Minister of Culture, Paris

1986
Issey Miyake als Titelgeschichte der Internationalen Ausgabe des Time Magazine vom 27. Januar

Zusammenarbeit mit dem Fotografen Irving Penn

Organisation der Ausstellung *HAATH, Handwoven Textiles in India and Issey Miyake.* Yurakucho Art Forum in Zusammenarbeit mit Seibu Museum of Art, Tokio

1987
Teilnahme an der Ausstellung *Fashion and Surrealism* des Fashion Institute of Technology, New York

1988
Issey Miyake A-ŪN, Ausstellung im Musée des Arts Décoratifs, Paris

Publikation von *Issey Miyake Photographs by Irving Penn*

Erhält den International Design Grand Award vom Japanese Cultural Design Council und den Ehrentitel Designer for Industry von der Royal Society of Art, London

Beginn seiner Arbeiten mit geknitterten, gefältelten Stoffen

1989
Issey Miyake Meets Lucie Rie, Ausstellung der Sogetsu Gallery, Tokio und des Museum of Oriental Ceramics, Osaka

Erhält den Mainichi Fashion Grand Prix

Collection pour hommes Printemps/Eté 1986 *Just a Moment* avec Patrick Dupond et les danseurs Momix au Centre Georges Pompidou, Paris

1986
Grand article sur Issey Miyake dans le magazine *Time,* édition internationale, le 27 janvier

Commence sa collaboration avec le photographe Irving Penn

Organise l'exposition *HAATH, Textiles tissés main en Inde et Issey Miyake* au Art Forum de Yurakucho en association avec le Musée d'Art de Seibu, Tokyo

1987
Participe à l'exposition *Fashion and Surrealism* au Fashion Institute of Technology, New York

1988
Exposition *Issey Miyake A-ŪN*, Musée des Arts Décoratifs, Paris

Publie le livre *Issey Miyake Photographs by Irving Penn*

Reçoit le Grand Prix International du Design décerné par le Conseil Culturel Japonais et le titre honorifique de Designer for Industry décerné par la Royal Society of Art, Londres

Commence à travailler sur les plissés

1989
Exposition *Issey Miyake Meets Lucie Rie*, Sogetsu Gallery, Tokyo, et Museum of Oriental Ceramics, Osaka

Reçoit le Mainichi Fashion Grand Prix

Issey Miyake A-ŪN poster
photograph © 1988 Irving Penn
designed by Ikko Tanaka, 1988

Issey Miyake Pleats Please poster
photograph © 1990 Irving Penn
designed by Ikko Tanaka, 1990

1990
Participated in a multi-media performance for the screening of the film *L'Inhumaine* (1923) by Marcel L'Herbier, Tokyo

Issey Miyake Pleats Please exhibition, Touko Museum of Contemporary Art, Tokyo

Participated in the exhibition *Energieën,* Stedelijk Museum, Amsterdam

Ten Sen Men exhibition, Hiroshima City Museum of Contemporary Art on the occasion of the first Hiroshima Art Prize

1991
Designed costumes for *The Loss of Small Detail* for the Frankfurt Ballet, choreographed by William Forsythe

Held the first self-sponsored lecture with Masashi Yamamura (Genshi-fu), Tokyo

Participated in the exhibition *Beyond Japan*, Barbican Art Gallery, London

Held the second self-sponsored lecture with Tadao Ando (Shiroishi-washi), Tokyo

1992
Received the Asahi Prize

Held the third self-sponsored lecture with Nakamura workshop (Kusakizome), Tokyo

Designed the uniforms for the Lithuanian team for the Olympic Games in Barcelona

Designed costumes for *As a Garden in this Setting* for the Frankfurt Ballet, choreographed by William Forsythe

Erhält den Orden Officier de l'Ordre des Arts et des Lettres von Jack Lang, Kulturminister, Paris

1990
Teilnahme an einer Multi-Media-Performance für den Film *L'Inhumaine* (1923) by Marcel L'Herbier, Tokio

Issey Miyake Pleats Please, Ausstellung am Touko Museum of Contemporary Art, Tokio

Mitwirkung an der Ausstellung *Energieën,* Stedelijk Museum, Amsterdam

Ten Sen Men, Ausstellung am Hiroshima City Museum of Contemporary Art anläßlich der Entgegennahme des ersten Hiroshima Art Prize

1991
Kostümentwürfe für *The Loss of Small Detail* für das Frankfurter Ballett, unter der Choreographie von William Forsythe

Erste Vorlesung, selbstfinanziert, mit Masashi Yamamura (Genshi-fu), Tokio

Teilnahme an der Ausstellung *Beyond Japan,* Barbican Art Gallery, London

Zweite Vorlesung mit Tadao Ando (Shiroishi-washi), Tokio

1992
Entgegennahme des Asahi Prize

Dritte, selbstgesponserte Vorlesung mit dem Nakamura Workshop (Kusakizome), Tokio

Entwirft die Kleidung der Litauischen Olympiadelegation für die Olympischen Spiele in Barcelona

Est fait Officier de l'Ordre des Arts et des Lettres par Jack Lang, Ministre de la Culture, Paris

1990
Participe à la représentation multi-media du film *L'Inhumaine* (1923) de Marcel L'Herbier, Tokyo

Exposition *Issey Miyake Pleats Please*, Touko Museum of Contemporary Art, Tokyo

Participe à l'Exposition *Energieën* , Musée Stedelijk, Amsterdam

Exposition *Ten Sen Men,* Hiroshima City Museum of Contemporary Art à l'occasion de la première remise d'un prix d'art par la ville

1991
Dessine les costumes pour le spectacle *The Loss of Small Detail* donné par le ballet de Francfort, avec une chorégraphie de William Forsythe

Donne sa première conférence autosponsorisée avec Masashi Yamamura (Genshi-fu) Tokyo

Participe à l'exposition *Beyond Japan* à la Barbican Art Gallery, Londres

Donne sa seconde conférence autosponsorisée avec Tadao Ando (Shiroishi-washi), Tokyo

1992
Reçoit le Prix Asahi

Donne sa troisième conférence autosponsorisée avec l'atelier Nakamura (Kusakizome), Tokyo

Dessine les uniformes des athlètes lituaniens pour les Jeux Olympiques de Barcelone

Ten Sen Men poster
photograph © 1990 Irving Penn
designed by Ikko Tanaka, 1990

Issey Miyake Twist poster
photograph © 1992 Irving Penn
designed by Ikko Tanaka, 1992

Issey Miyake Twist exhibition, Naoshima Contemporary Art Museum, Kagawa

Held the fourth self-sponsored lecture with Akiko Ishigaki and Amanda Mayer Stinchecum, Tokyo

Launched *L'Eau d'Issey* perfume

1993
Pleats Please Issey Miyake line established

Designed uniforms for staff of the Japanese Pavilion at the Taejon International Exposition, Korea

Received the Chevalier de l'Ordre National de la Légion d'Honneur from the French Government, Paris

Received honorary Doctorate from the Royal Collage of Art, London

Received The Mainichi Fashion Grand Prix

Issey Miyake Moves, a documentary film broadcast on WOWOW, Japan

Gave the Blackburn Lecture *Pushing the Boundaries* at Central Saint Martin's College of Art and Design

1994
Autumn/Winter 1994/95 collection in Tokyo using three-dimensional video

Invited by The School of the Art Institute of Chicago to give a lecture

Invited by The New York Public Library to give a lecture at Celeste Bartos Forum, New York

Kostümentwürfe für *As a Garden in this Setting* für das Frankfurter Ballett choreographiert von William Forsythe

Issey Miyake Twist, Ausstellung in Naoshima Contemporary Art Museum, Kagawa

Vierte, selbstgesponserte Vorlesung mit Akiko Ishigaki und Amanda Mayer Stinchecum, Tokio

Lanciert *L'Eau d'Issey* Parfum

1993
Einführung der Kollektion *Pleats Please Issey Miyake*

Entwirft die Hostessen-Uniformen für den Japanischen Pavillon der Taejon International Exposition, Korea

Wird mit dem Orden Chevalier de l'Ordre National de la Légion d'Honneur von der französischen Regierung ausgezeichnet

Ehrendoktorat des Royal College of Art, London

Erhält den Mainichi Fashion Grand Prix

Dokumentarfilm *Issey Miyake Moves,* gezeigt vom japanischen Fernsehsender WOWOW

Pushing the Boundaries (Grenzen überwinden), Blackburn-Vorlesung am Saint Martin's College of Art and Design, London

1994
Herbst/Winterkollektion 1994/95 Vorführung mit dreidimensionalem Video in Tokio

Vorlesung am Art Institute of Chicago

Einladung der New Yorker Public Library, eine Vorlesung am Celeste Bartos Forum in New York

Dessine les costumes du Ballet de Francfort *As a Garden in this Setting* avec chorégraphie de William Forsythe

Exposition *Issey Miyake Twist,* Contemporary Art Museum de Naoshima, Kagawa

Donne sa quatrième conférence autosponsorisée avec Akiko Ishigaki et Amanda Mayer Stinchecum, Tokyo

Lance le parfum *L'Eau d'Issey*

1993
Création de la ligne *Pleats Please Issey Miyake*

Dessine les uniformes du personnel du pavillon japonais à l'Exposition Internationale de Taejon, en Corée

Reçoit l'ordre de Chevalier de l'Ordre National de la Légion d'Honneur du gouvernement français.

Devient docteur honoris causa du Royal College of Art, Londres

Reçoit le Grand Prix de la mode de Mainichi

Issey Miyke Moves, documentaire diffusé sur la chaîn WOWOW, Japan

Donne la conférence de Blackburn: *Pushing the Boundaries* (Franchir les démarcations) au Central Saint Martin's College of Art and Design, Londres

1994
Collection Automne/Hiver 1994/95 à Tokyo utilisant des images vidéo en trois dimensions

Invité à l'Art Institute de Chicago pour y donner une conférence

Conférence au Celeste Bartos Forum, à l'invitation de la New York Public Library

BIBLIOGRAPHY

ISSEY MIYAKE 三宅一生の発想と展開 East Meets West

Books

Issey Miyake East Meets West
designed by Ikko Tanaka
edited by Kazuko Koike, Heibonsha, 1978

Issey Miyake Bodyworks
Shogakukan, Tokyo, 1983

*Issey Miyake & Miyake Design Studio
1970–1985.*
Obunsha, Tokyo, 1985

Issey Miyake: Photographs by Irving Penn
layout by Irving Penn
New York Graphic Society Books in association with
Callaway Editions in U.S., Edipresse-Livres S.A.
in France, and Libro Port Publishing Co.
Ltd. in Japan, 1988

Issey Miyake by Irving Penn 1989
designed by Ikko Tanaka
Miyake Design Studio, Tokyo, 1989
Limited Edition

Issey Miyake by Irving Penn 1990
designed by Ikko Tanaka
Miyake Design Studio, Tokyo, 1990
Limited Edition

Issey Miyake by Irving Penn 1991–92
designed by Ikko Tanaka
Miyake Design Studio, Tokyo, 1990, 1991
Limited Edition

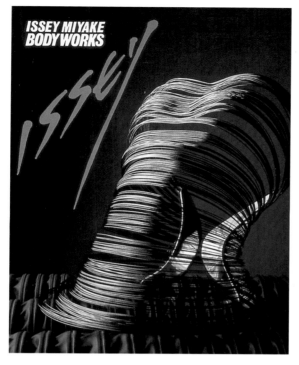 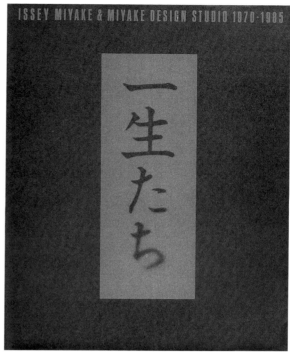

Selected
Catalogues:

A Poem of Cloth and Stone
Tokyo, 1963

Fly with Issey Miyake
Tokyo, 1977

MA: Espace-Temps du Japon
Musée des Arts Décoratifs
Paris 1978

Les Tissus imprimés d'Issey Miyake
Musée de L'Impression sur Étoffes de
Mulhouse, France, 1979

Issey Miyake: It's so Neat
Tokyo, 1981

Issey and Kenzo
Tokyo, 1982

Intimate Architecture:
Contemporary Clothing Design
M.I.T., 1982

Issey Miyake Bodyworks: Fashion Without
Taboos
Victoria and Albert Museum
London, 1985

Issey Miyake by Tadanori Yokoo
Okanoyama Museum of Art
Nishiwaki, 1985

Les Textiles de L'Inde
Musée des Arts Décoratifs
Paris, 1985

HAATH, Handwoven Textiles
in India and Issey Miyake
Seibu Museum of Art
Tokyo, 1986

Energieën
Stedelijk Museum
Amsterdam, 1990

Issey Miyake Pleats Please
Touko Museum of Contemporary Art
Tokyo, 1990

Ten Sen Men
Hiroshima City Museum, 1990

Beyond Japan
Barbican Art Gallery
London, 1991

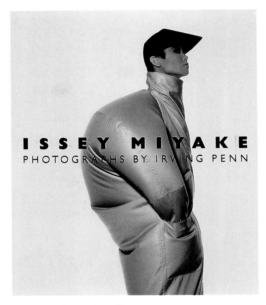

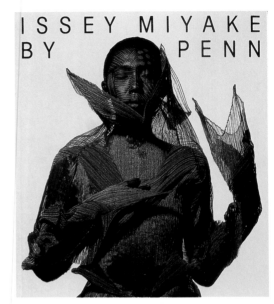

photograph © 1988 Irving Penn   photograph © 1989 Irving Penn

Selected
Articles:

Elle
Paris
September 10, 1973

Artforum
New York
Out of the East
A Rising Star
Anna Wintour
March 22, 1982

Time
Into the Soul of Fabric
Jay Cocks
August 1, 1983

Newsweek
Miyake's Fashion Revolution
Douglas Davis
October 17, 1983

New Yorker
The Great Monument, Profile
Kennedy Fraser
December 18, 1983

Time Out
London
The Art Of Clothing
Steve Grant
February 28, 1985

Time
The Man Who's Changing Clothes
Designer Issey Miyake Makes Fashion for Tomorrow
Issey Miyake, Jay Cocks
International Edition
October 21, 1985
Asian Edition January 27, 1986

Elle
Paris
1970–1986: Le phénomène Issey Miyake
Francine Vormese
February 3, 1986

Frankfurter Allgemeine Zeitung
Magazin
Issey Miyake
Irmtraud Schaarschmidt-Richter
April 11, 1986

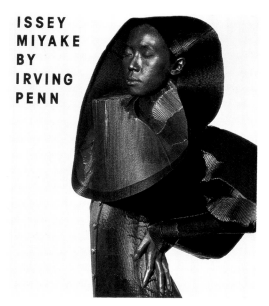

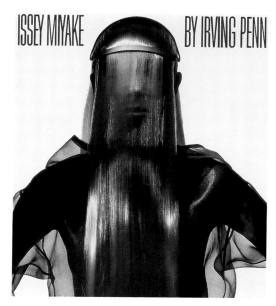

photograph © 1989 Irving Penn

photograph © 1991 Irving Penn

Connaissance des Arts
Paris
Issey Miyake
Le plus sculpteur des couturiers
Gilles Néret
March 1987

Artforum
New York
Image of a Second Skin
Mark Holborn
November 1988

Elle
London
Modern Master
Sally Brompton
June 1989

Interview
New York
Pleats Please
Ingrid Sischy
September 1990

Frankfurter Allgemeine Zeitung
Issey Miyake: Mode Zum Tanzen Gebracht
Maria Franziska Adelman
July 5, 1991

New Yorker
Issey Does It
Michael Gross
July 22, 1991

Süddeutsche Zeitung Magazin
Zukunftsmodelle
Hans-Christoph Blumenberg
January 15, 1993

Page 154 · Seite 154
Bouncing Dress
Spring/Summer 1993
Photo: Rainer Leitzgen for
Süddeutsche Zeitung Magazin

Page 155 · Seite 155
Pleats & Twist
Spring/Summer 1993
Photo: Rainer Leitzgen for
Süddeutsche Zeitung Magazin

Page 157 · Seite 157
Cotton Cocoon Dress
Spring/Summer 1993
Photo: Rainer Leitzgen for
Süddeutsche Zeitung Magazin

Acknowledgements · Danksagung · Remerciements

This book would have been impossible without the attention of Midori Kitamura to every detail of the design and text. Her colleagues at the Miyake Design Studio in Tokyo, Masako Omori and Michiko Katsura, have been tireless in their support. I am also very grateful to Jun Kanai of the New York office of the Miyake Design Studio.

Angelika Muthesius, Silvia Krieger and Susanne Rödder have managed to keep the triangle of communication between London, Cologne and Tokyo functioning with grace and efficiency, for which I offer my thanks.

Above all, I am indebted to Issey Miyake for his generosity and inspiration at all times.

Mark Holborn

Issey Miyake
Photo: Hiro

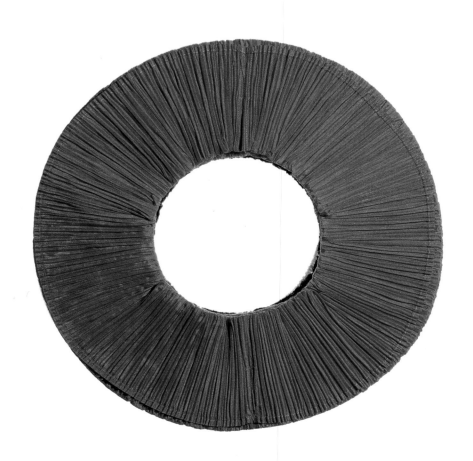